What People Are Saying  About Our Books

"Trusting a recipe often comes down to trusting the source.
The sources for the recipes are impeccable;
in fact, they're some of the best chefs in the nation."
Bon Appetit Magazine

"Should be in the library—and kitchen—of every serious cook."
Jim Wood—Food and Wine Editor—San Francisco Examiner

"A well-organized and user-friendly tribute to
many of the state's finest restaurant chefs."
San Francisco Chronicle

"An attractive guide to the best restaurants and inns,
offering recipes from their delectable repertoire of menus."
Gail Rudder Kent—Country Inns Magazine

"Outstanding Cookbook"
Heritage Newspapers

"I couldn't decide whether to reach for my telephone and make reservations
or reach for my apron and start cooking."
James McNair—Best-selling cookbook author

"It's an answer to what to eat, where to eat—and how to do it yourself."
The Herald

"I dare you to browse through these recipes
without being tempted to rush to the kitchen."
Pat Griffith—Chief, Washington Bureau, Blade Communications, Inc.

The Elegant Martini

Celebrating Seductive Recipes for Appetizers and Libations

KATHLEEN DeVANNA FISH

BON VIVANT

Library of Congress Cataloging-in-Publication Data

THE ELEGANT MARTINI

Celebrating Seductive Recipes for Appetizers and Libations

Fish, Kathleen DeVanna

97-071564

ISBN 1-883214-13-0

$17.95 softcover

Includes indexes

Autobiography page

Copyright ©1998 by Kathleen DeVanna Fish

Cover photograph by Robert N. Fish

Editorial direction by Charlotte D. Atkins, Lisa Crawford Watson, and
  Judie Marks

Editorial assistance by Nadine Guarrera

Cover design by Morris Design

Interior by Cimarron Design

Published by Bon Vivant Press,
a division of The Millennium Publishing Group
P.O. Box 1994
Monterey, CA 93942

Printed in the United States of America

Contents

The Elegant Martini

THERE WAS A TIME WHEN ELEGANT, COUPLED WITH MARTINI, would have been redundant. When anyone who knew how to make a martini was upper crust, and anyone who knew how to swill a martini, deserved one. You had to be old enough, successful enough and dashing enough to serve one; pretty enough to accept it; and sophisticated enough to consume it. There was a look, a pace, a ritual and a message, and anyone who was anyone knew it.

We like to pretend it was a simpler era, when ladies sipped tea and dames swilled vodka. Women threw more curves with their femininity than their feminism. It was a period when men and women wore hats; when a martini and a cigarette fit in one hand, leaving the other one free for meaningful conversation.

It was a time extended by the silver screen, which gave permission and purpose to the martini through several significant scenes: When Cary Grant and Deborah Kerr toasted one another in "An Affair to Remember" (1957), or Ernest Hemingway and the inimitable Marlene Dietrich glanced soulfully at one another at the Stork Club in New York.

"The name's Bond...James Bond. I'll have a dry martini; three measures of Gordon's, one of vodka, half a measure of Kina Lillet. Shake it, do not stir it, until it's ice cold, then add a large, thin slice of lemon peel. Got it?"

Hollywood moved into the financial district, and the three-martini power lunch became standard operating procedure for business in the '50s, '60s, '70s...Is it really over?

All of these images are accurate, but none of them are real. Except, of course, for the martini itself and, likely, the triple-swill lunch.

Unquestionably, the martini is still the ultimate American drink, still the standard for our sophistication; even more so, our elegance. It is an icon that shook up the California Gold Rush, thrived through Prohibition, survived Jimmy Carter's vow to eradicate the three-martini lunch from the proverbial expense account and superseded the American obsession with health and denial.

Today, the martini once again reigns as the social standard, in supper clubs and martini bars across the country; where the elite, the not-so-elite, and the don't-care-about-elite meet to eat, drink and greet Mary…

Although the beginnings of the martini are hotly or, in some cases, coolly contested, it all began on a dark and stormy night somewhere between San Francisco's Occidental Hotel—where a truly legendary bartender named "Professor" Jerry Thomas is said to have invented the drink for a questionable traveler on his way to Martinez, California—and the Ferry Street saloon in Martinez, itself, where owner Julio Richelieu is said to have balanced the scales when a miner threw down gold nuggets, with an invention he christened "the Martinez Cocktail."

What is documented, is that by the 1880s, Richelieu was serving the "Martinez" at Lotta's Fountain on the corner of Kearny and Market streets in San Francisco, while the professor was shaking and stirring—and publishing a recipe for—much the same blend of cocktail on the opposite coast in Manhattan. Makes you wonder who created the "Manhattan."

Early martinis were a far cry from the dry martini that has become the libation of choice for more than three generations of Americans spanning the current century. A popular recipe from 1887 called for one dash bitters, two dashes of maraschino syrup, one wineglass of vermouth, two small lumps of ice, one pony of Old Tom gin (a sweetened product of London) and a quarter slice of lemon, as well as the provision: "If the guest prefers it very sweet, add two dashes of gum syrup."

The word "martini," as a descriptive term for a cocktail, made it to the Oxford Dictionary by 1894; the same year the Heublein Company marketed a pre-mixed martini. Two years later in 1896, Thomas Stuart published a recipe for a drink he called the "Marguerite," which is almost identical to the dry

The word "martini," as a descriptive term for a cocktail, made it to the Oxford Dictionary by 1894

martini: 1 dash of orange bitters, ⅔ measure of Plymouth gin (Unlike Old Tom, this was a dry gin), and ⅓ measure of French vermouth.

Gin first arrived in the United States accompanied by Dutch settlers, but it trailed whisky and brandy in popularity until the end of the 19th century. Vermouth was virtually unknown until the invention of the martini.

By 1904, the martini had become a popular literary device, first mentioned by O. Henry in "The Gentle Grafter." Since then, it has been a stand-by, both widely consumed and written about by such literary legends as Jack London, Ogden Nash, Ernest Hemingway, Noël Coward, E.B. White, Dorothy Parker, Robert Benchley, Ian Fleming, Russell Baker and Luis Buñel, to honor but a few.

Whether art imitates life or life mirrors art, America's love affair with the martini reflects its romance with the silver screen. Previously mentioned scenes of promise and passion in "An Affair to Remember," the drama of "Casino Royale," and the intrigue of "Dr. No" and "Goldfinger" merely set the stage.

Yet the history of the martini is well recorded in much earlier annals of cinematography. Those who can remember will likely never forget the importance of martinis in films like "China Seas" with Clarke Gable and Jean Harlow; that wonderful old private-eye series, "The Thin Man," where Nick Charles was portrayed by William Powell, and his wife Nora, first by Maureen O'Sullivan and later, by Myrna Loy; or David Niven in "My Man Godfrey." In "Auntie Mame," Rosalind Russell and Willard Waterman shared a couple of dry ones, and Joan Crawford glared from behind her stirred martini in "Humoresque." Of course she did. And there were more…

The most dramatic use of the martini as a cinematic device undoubtedly occurred in the Academy Award-winning "All About Eve," when Bette Davis turned to martinis to hold back the hands of time.

W.C. Fields drank martinis for breakfast and consumed two quarts of gin a day. William Holden had a private martini bar in his dressing room. Frank Sinatra and David Wayne proposed martini toasts in "The Tender Trap," and Luis Buñel wrote a scene to extol the snobbery of the martini society in "The Discreet Charm of the Bourgeoisie." Martini glamour was really no greater then than it is now; it was simply more discreet; as all indiscretions were, then.

The martini has invaded many aspects of our public and private lives, as has politics. Franklin D. Roosevelt plied Stalin with martinis at the 1943 Tehran Conference while Nikita Khrushchev acknowledged the martini as "America's lethal weapon." Sir Winston Churchill's idea of a dry martini was to pour gin into a pitcher and "glance briefly at a bottle of vermouth across the room."

President Jimmy Carter, who caused a temporary wagon ride when he forbade alcoholic beverages in the White House, said, "As for the famous three-martini lunch, I don't care how many martinis anyone has with lunch, but I am concerned about who picks up the tab."

But the late 1980s beckoned the return of the martini romance—in houses both public and private. Plenty of Reaganites imbibed. The Bush administration drank vodka martinis, shaken and served straight up with a twist of lemon. Martinis are not popular in the Clinton house, but this hasn't stopped the martini from persisting as the cocktail of choice among a generation of aging Baby Boomer Americans, many of whom consider it a patriotic totem…as a symbol of what, is as individual as the consumer and the recipe. Although vodka may have replaced gin as the preferred base for some, vermouth is still in the mix, as is the almighty olive and the lemon peel.

We are pleased to continue the celebration with *The Elegant Martini,* as we present, in all their glory, some of the most popular martini recipes from across the country, as well as savory appetizers to accompany them—all of which have been perfected and served by some of the most elegant establishments in the nation.

Prepare to be tempted. Plan to partake. And, by all means, *do* try this at home.

Sir Winston Churchill's idea of a dry martini was to pour gin into a pitcher and "glance briefly at a bottle of vermouth across the room."

Menu of Martinis

Absolut Sensation	Compass Rose 85
Absolutly Fabulous	The Martini Club 85
All Too Important Martini	Johnny Love's 76
Antini	Harry Denton's Starlight Room 85
Blue Sapphire	The Mandarin 76
Blue Skyy Martini	Compass Rose 86
Cajun Martini	Compass Rose 86
Campton Cosmo	Campton Place Hotel 86
Campton Cure	Campton Place Hotel 88
Cardinal Sin	Garden Court at The Four Seasons Olympic Hotel 88
Champagne Royale de Martini	Tongue & Groove 88
Chesapeake Martini	Explorer's Club 89
Chocolate Martini	Johnny Love's 89
Citrus Brandy Martini	Pravda 89
Citrus Martini	Compass Rose 90
Classic Dry	The Martini Club 77
Classic Extra Dry	The Martini Club 77
Classic Old Fashioned Martini	The Lenox Room 77
Classic Sapphire	The Covey at Quail Lodge Resort & Golf Club 78
Contemporary	The Covey at Quail Lodge Resort & Golf Club 90
Copper Illusion	Garden Court at The Four Seasons Olympic Hotel 78
Cosmopolitan	Top of the Hub 90
Dark Crystal	Compass Rose 91
Diamond Martini	Compass Rose 92
Dirty Gin Martini	Johnny Love's 78

Dirty Martini	The Martini Club 92
Dirty Vodka Martini	Tongue & Groove 92
Dog Bites Back	The Martini Club 93
Double White Chocolate Martini	Mumbo Jumbo 93
Dutch Martini	The Martini Club 93
Framboise Martini	San Ysidro Ranch 94
Frangelico Martini	Pravda 94
French Martini	Pravda 94
Fuzzy Martini	Club 36 95
Georgia Peach	The Martini Club 95
Gibson Martini	Johnny Love's 80
Ginseng Martini	Le Colonial 95
Glacier Blue	Garden Court at The Four Seasons Olympic Hotel 112
Grand Martini	Tongue & Groove 96
Grand Vodka Martini	The Martini Club 96
Harry's Martini	Harry Denton's Starlight Room 80
Jamaican Martini	The Martini Club 114
James Bond	The Martini Club 112
James Bond Martini	The Ritz-Carlton Bar at The Ritz-Carlton 96
Julip Martini	Mason's Restaurant 110
Knickerbocker Martini	The Rainbow Room 80
Kurant Chocolate Martini	Campton Place Hotel 98
Kurant Cosmopolitan	Compass Rose 98
Lady Godiva	The Martini Club 98
Lemon Cosmopolitan	The Martini Club 99
Lemon Drop Martini	Tongue & Groove 99
Lenox Room Peachy Keen Martini	The Lenox Room 99

Menu of Appetizers

Appetizer and Martini Pairings

Barbecued Duck Taco with Tomatillo Salsa—*San Ysidro Ranch*
Dog Bites Back—The Martini Club

Basil Pesto Dip with Crackers—*Vegetarian Pleasures*
Classic Old Fashioned Martini—The Lenox Room

Bay Scallops and Mandarin Orange Skewers—*Flerchinger's Vineyards*
Fuzzy Martini—Club 36

Blue Cheese Meatballs—*Yakima River Winery*
Very Dirty Martini—Pravda

Bruschetta with Gorgonzola and Walnuts—*Galileo*
Traditional Martini—Harry Denton's Starlight Room

Ceviche of Striped Bass and Scallops—*Compass Rose*
Veloz Martini—San Ysidro Ranch

Chicken Drumsticks with Merlot and Blackberries—*Yakima River Winery*
Razamataz—Club XIX

Chicken Kabobs—*Compass Rose*
Night Shift Martini—Club 36

Country Pâté—*Chinzombo Safari Lodge*
All Too Important Martini—Johnny Love's

Crab Meat Spring Roll and Tamari Sauce—*Top of the Hub*
Pure Martini—The Ritz-Carlton Bar at The Ritz-Carlton

Crispy Pan-Fried Oysters—*Pravda*
Copper Illusion—Garden Court at The Four Seasons Olympic Hotel

Eggplant Caviar—*Bayona*
The 007–Shaken, not Stirred—The Viper Room

Ethiopian Chicken Legs—*Chinzombo Safari Lodge*
Lemon Cosmopolitan—The Martini Club

Goat Cheese Spring Rolls—*Kaspar's*
Patsy's Martini—The Martini Club

Honeyed Teriyaki Chicken Nuggets—*Tefft Cellars*
Melon-Collie—The Mandarin

Italian White Bean Cakes—*Chez Shea*
Dog Bites Back—The Martini Club

Jasmine Tea Smoked Salmon Buckwheat Blini and Asian Salad—*Club 36*
Ginseng Martini—Le Colonial

Lobster and Corn Fritters—*Arrows*
Champagne Royale de Martini—Tongue & Groove

Lobster in Mango Cups—*Tommy Toy's*
Tropical Martini—Mason's Restaurant

Pineapple Rum Martini—*The Martini Club*
Lobster Tamale—San Ysidro Ranch

Campton Cure—*Campton Place Hotel*
Maine Crab Cakes—Christian's

Whisky Manhattan—*The Martini Club*
Oyster Six Shot—Palace Café

Chesapeake Martini—*Explorer's Club*
Oysters in Champagne Sauce—Chinzombo Safari Lodge

Patsy's Martini—*The Martini Club*
Champagne Royale de Martini—Tongue & Groove

Peppered Halibut Gravlax with Vodka—*Compass Rose*
Mumbo Martini—Mumbo Jumbo

Pesto and Prosciutto Palmiers—*Chinzombo Safari Lodge*
Skyy Scraper—The Martini Club

Potstickers with Lobster in Three Dipping Sauces—*Arrows*
Tropical Martini—Mason's Restaurant

Ricotta Cheese and Figs in Grape Leaves—*Mixx, An American Bistro*
Park Avenue—Johnny Love's

Rotolo di Prosciutto and Formaggi—*Chinzombo Safari Lodge*
Perfect Martini—Johnny Love's

Rouge et Noir Brie Quiche—*La Gare*
Grand Martini—Tongue & Groove

Samoosas—*Chinzombo Safari Lodge*
The 24-Karrot Martini—Compass Rose

Satay Sticks—*Chinzombo Safari Lodge*
Cosmopolitan—Top of the Hub

Seared Scallop and Duck Foie Gras on Caramelized Maui Pineapple—*Top of the Hub*
Pineapple Rum Martini—The Martini Club

Shrimp with Prosciutto di Parma—*Ciao Europa*
Kurant Cosmopolitan—Compass Rose

Skillet Roasted Mussels Flamed In Lemon-Anise Infused Vodka—*Infusion Bar & Restaurant*
Campton Cure—Campton Place Hotel

Small Red Potatoes Stuffed with Smoked Trout Mousse and Caviar—*Post Ranch Inn*
Knickerbocker Martini—The Rainbow Room

Smoked Salmon—*Garden Court at the Four Seasons Olympic Hotel*
Yang Martini—Inagiku

Smoked Salmon Pinwheels—*The Covey at Quail Lodge Resort & Golf Club*
Classic Dry—The Martini Club

Smoked Trout Sandwich with Lemon Dill Mayonnaise—*Pravda*
Thin Man Martini—The Rainbow Room

Spicy Orange Shrimp—*Chinzombo Safari Lodge*
Fuzzy Martini—Club 36

Springroll with Beet Vinaigrette—*San Ysidro Ranch*
Ying Martini—Inagiku

Stuffed Morel Mushrooms—*The Covey at Quail Lodge Resort & Golf Club*
Diamond Martini—Compass Rose

Tapenade—*Bayona*
Dirty Vodka Martini—Tongue & Groove

Tender Corn Pancake with Salmon and Golden Caviar—*Club XIX at the Lodge at Pebble Beach*
Limonnaya Martini—The Martini Club

Thai Crab Cakes—*Flying Fish*
Tropical Martini—Mason's Restaurant

Vegetable Spring Rolls—*Providence*
Melon Vodka Martini—Compass Rose

Wild Mushroom Crostini—*Explorer's Club*
Vodka Martini—Johnny Love's

Wild Mushroom Quesadilla with Herbed Cheese—*Compass Rose*
Cajun Martini—Compass Rose

Won Ton with Crab Meat and Chives—*Tommy Toy's*
Absolutly Fabulous—The Martini Club

Won Tons Stuffed with Shrimp, Pork, Water Chestnut & Wood Ear Mushrooms—*Le Colonial*
Mr. Phat's Citrus Martini—The Viper Room

Martini Stars

CAMPTON PLACE HOTEL 22
340 Stockton Street ▪ San Francisco, CA ▪ (415) 781-5555

CLUB XIX 25
The Lodge at Pebble Beach
2700 Seventeen-Mile Drive ▪ Pebble Beach, CA ▪ (408) 625-8519

CLUB 36 27
Grand Hyatt San Francisco
345 Stockton Street ▪ San Francisco, CA ▪ (415) 398-1234

COMPASS ROSE 29
The Westin St. Francis
335 Powell Street ▪ San Francisco, CA ▪ (415) 774-0167

EXPLORER'S CLUB 31
Harbor Court Hotel
550 Light Street ▪ Baltimore, MD ▪ (410) 234-0550

THE GARDEN COURT 33
Four Seasons Olympic Hotel
411 University Street ▪ Seattle, WA ▪ (206) 621-1700

HARRY DENTON'S STARLIGHT ROOM 35
Sir Francis Drake Hotel
450 Powell Street, 21st Floor   San Francisco, CA   (415) 395-8595

INFUSION BAR AND RESTAURANT 37
555 Second Street ▪ San Francisco, CA ▪ (415) 543-2282

JOHNNY LOVE'S 40
1500 Broadway ▪ San Francisco, CA ▪ (415) 931-8021

LE COLONIAL 42
8783 Beverly Boulevard ▪ West Hollywood, CA ▪ (310) 289-0660

THE LENOX ROOM 44
1278 Third Avenue ▪ New York City, NY ▪ (212) 772-0404

THE MANDARIN RESTAURANT 47
Ghirardelli Square
900 North Point ▪ San Francisco, CA ▪ (415) 673-8812

THE MARTINI CLUB 48
1140 Crescent Avenue ▪ Atlanta, GA ▪ (404) 873-0794

MUMBO JUMBO 50
89 Park Place ▪ Atlanta, GA ▪ (404) 523-0330

PRAVDA 54
281 Lafayette Street ▪ New York City, NY ▪ (212) 226-4696

THE RAINBOW ROOM 57
30 Rockefeller Plaza, 65th Floor   New York, N.Y.   (212) 632-5000

RITZ-CARLTON BAR 61
The Ritz-Carlton San Francisco
600 Stockton Street ▪ San Francisco, CA ▪ (415) 296-7465

SAN YSIDRO RANCH 64
900 San Ysidro Lane ▪ Santa Barbara, CA ▪ (805) 969-5046

TONGUE & GROOVE 67
3055 Peachtree Road N.E. ▪ Atlanta, GA ▪ (404) 261-2325

TOP OF THE HUB 69
Prudential Tower
800 Boylston Street ▪ Boston, MA ▪ (617) 536-1775

THE VIPER ROOM 72
8852 Sunset Boulevard ▪ West Hollywood, CA ▪ (310) 358-1881

Bars

Campton Place Hotel

$\mathcal{A}$ simple brownstone facade with an even simpler white awning. The only chance they stand of enticing you in is their reputation which, in the case of Campton Place, precedes itself as the city's "most romantic hotel" and as having "one of the most romantic dining rooms in the city." Which, for San Francisco, says a lot.

The romance is likely attributed to the interior decor of a stately hotel whose quiet and luxurious accommodations over-look a verdant atrium——and a restaurant whose intimate and elegant setting sparks the mood for a night to remember.

"Special," inherent in romantic, is credited to Executive Chef Todd Humphries, who is committed to refuting two long-standing beliefs about gourmet dining: "…that hotels can't compete with the country's finest restaurants; and that a master chef simply doesn't have time to create a special dish at a moment's notice."

Humphries rises to the occasion on a daily basis with an award-winning menu whose main feature is an unwritten "if you don't see it, ask for it" policy. He actually welcomes the challenge to create a special order under pressure; though most guests find his broad and tantalizing offerings to be more than enough to satisfy their tastes.

The twist that brings 'em in mid-week is "Martini Night" in the hotel lounge. Wednesday nights feature specially priced martinis and live music, both of which entice myriad regulars to their favorite downtown watering hole.

The dining room may seduce the palate, but the Campton Place bartenders go all the way with anything from a *Classic Dry*

340 STOCKTON STREET

SAN FRANCISCO, CA

(415) 781-5555

Martini to the signature *Chocolate Martini* originally created for Valentine's Day. For those looking for an antidote to the status quo, the *Campton Cure* upgrades a traditional *Cosmopolitan* by replacing vodka with Absolut Citron Vodka, and triple sec with Cointreau. "It gives the drink a fruitier, more refined flavor," says Campton Place bartender Michael Grohman.

According to Grohman, "Old-fashioned drinks are coming back into fashion, but don't be afraid to ask us to create something special. Who knows? Maybe that creation will be the next new trend."

And rest assured that Chef Humphries is keeping up with the evolution of Grohman's sophisticated libations with his designer bar menu of complementary hors d'oeuvres.

Club XIX

SOME SAY we owe the spectacular beauty of Pebble Beach to Mother Nature; others contend the credit belongs to Samuel F.B. Morse—or at least, perhaps, the preservation of its natural gifts as it developed into a haven for some of the finest scenery, golf and glamorous living in the world.

He also understood the beauty of a good dry martini. Had Club XIX at The Lodge at Pebble Beach existed during the reign of the legendary developer, surely it would have been his signature spot to sip his favorite martini.

With an address like the scenic Seventeen-Mile Drive and stellar views of Carmel Bay, Club XIX at The Lodge at Pebble Beach is both a natural and luxurious place in which to dine and enjoy cocktails.

The Lodge's reputation for relaxed elegance amid a stunning natural bounty is world-renowned.

Of course, when famed Chef Hubert Keller, co-owner of San Francisco's Fleur de Lys, added his expertise and signature to the restaurant, Club XIX took on a French flair of its own, implementing a lighter approach to haute cuisine executed by Pebble Beach Chef Lisa Magadini. Diners are treated to a feast

ᛒᚷ

THE LODGE AT PEBBLE BEACH

2700 SEVENTEEN-MILE DRIVE

PEBBLE BEACH, CA

(408) 625-8519

for the senses in an intimate setting evoking the charm of fine Parisian restaurants, dining against an endless Pacific backdrop.

On Club XIX's bricked patio, romantic fireplaces warm and coastal views inspire lingering meals and respites adjacent to the 18th green of Pebble Beach's famed golf links.

While The Lodge at Pebble Beach is a true classic where martini lovers can certainly find themselves sipping a classic dry one, Club XIX bartenders are eager to tempt taste buds with a few designer martinis of their own, such as the *Peaches & Cream*. And like an Erica Jong poem, *The Razamataz* leaves you with a new appreciation of raspberries.

Club 36

REST ASSURED that the Hyatt on Union Square has just about everything its guests could hope for, from spectacular San Francisco skyline and bay views, to designer rooms, state-of-the-art business accommodations, fully equipped fitness facilities and in-your-dreams shopping. It's their business to indulge their guests, and they're very good at it.

So why not also have one of the sexiest, most indulgent rooftop lounges that hosts panoramic views, world-renowned jazz musicians and libations worth ascending for. Exactly.

Rising 36 stories above the Grand Hyatt, Club 36 covers the top half of the hotel and looks out on thousands of twinkling city lights. The spacious lounge is accented with an oversized bar, a baby grand piano, lush black leather chairs, chrome, smoke-gray marble tables, twin sculpted iron chandeliers and rich carpet.

GRAND HYATT SAN FRANCISCO
345 STOCKTON STREET
SAN FRANCISCO, CA
(415) 398-1234

*The Grand Hyatt
overlooking Union Square*

A highlight is that the skyward lounge plays host to renowned jazz musician Larry Vuckovich five nights a week. Vuckovich has toured the world and is regarded as one of the most versatile pianists in jazz circles today. He's performed with Dexter Gordon, Bobby McFerrin, Pete Escovedo and Mel Torme.

Even though the sky is the limit if you want a cocktail at the Hyatt, you don't always have to venture to the 36th floor.

The Plaza Bar is an intimate enclave nestled within the hotel's Plaza Restaurant, with feel-good leather bar stools, marble accents and soft lighting.

The atmosphere is actually more casual than the setting or the beverages, both at once contemporary and classic, featuring drinks on the stem, blended cocktails, premium California wines and after-dinner cordials.

The restaurant, designed in the tradition of a grand California café, boasts elegant floor-to-ceiling windows over-looking historic Union Square; and golden rattan furniture softened with lush live palms.

While you could create an indulgent San Francisco experience without ever leaving the hotel, you might want to venture out to the square, ride a cable car, eat a crab cocktail on the Wharf. Club 36 and The Plaza Bar will be waiting with a chilled glass and a little jazz to top off your day.

Compass Rose

Having been dubbed "the most beautiful room in the world," the Compass Rose has long been the place to rendezvous in the city's landmark Union Square area.

Inspired by the interior of the Cluny Museum in Paris, the room at the corner of Powell and Geary streets in San Francisco is adorned with fluted columns framing high, ornate ceilings with exotic orchids and crystal lamps suspended there and enclosed in rich wood-paneled walls.

Of course, the St. Francis hotel, which houses the renowned Compass Rose, has provided its own source of inspiration for travelers from around the world since 1904.

Many a theatergoer or traveler has enjoyed champagne and caviar or the house specialty—martinis—amid the unusual objets d'art that adorn the classic room.

Designer Joszi Meskan and her staff scoured the world for art, artifacts and antiques to conjure up the stately character this world-class hotel has grown to represent. Stately, however, does not mean stuffy. There's a good deal of eclectic charm to be appreciated here as well.

"The room is colorful and lively," says Meskan, "but it's also subtly wicked with a touch of decadence."

THE WESTIN ST. FRANCIS

335 POWELL STREET

SAN FRANCISCO, CA

(415) 774-0167

Custom-designed furniture is framed by handsome paneling and an open-beamed ceiling all carved from solid oak. Access to this elegant salon is via a sweeping staircase of Italian verde marble. The same marble trims the dramatic arched windows, draped in hand-painted raw silk, that expose a charming view of cable cars tooling up and down Powell Street.

Vintage treasures include a pair of sofas, covered in sinful red satin with carved bases, rescued from the fire at Brighton Pavilion. Other seats, including a few tête-à-têtes for intimate conversation, are piled with pillows made from heirloom Chinese robes and ceremonial garments.

The room's main bar is topped with polished walnut and supported by a pair of hand-carved white marble griffins. Wooden chairs with carved swan-head armrests afford plenty of bar seating. Lamp shades were painted by local artists while framed Chinese embroideries hang on the walls along with modern prints from the hotel's collection. Eye-catching and artful screens not only serve as intriguing artwork, but also help divide the spacious room into more intimate sections.

A red-and-green marble dance floor gets ample use since there's nightly entertainment by the Abe Battat Trio, a gig that's been an institution at the St. Francis for more than 25 years.

Celebrity customers have included Christopher Reeve, Burt Reynolds, Lana Turner, Telly Savalas, June Lockhart, Greg Allman and Rita Moreno. Andy Garcia once joined Battat's band for a set on the bongo drums.

Even with such star-caliber clientele, the Compass Room itself still demands center stage. After all, a rose by any other name...

Explorer's Club

LIFE-SIZE ELEPHANTS and monkeys silhouetted at dusk draw you into the trompe l'oeil safari. If you focus on John Wullbrandt's heroic African-inspired mural long enough, you'll likely linger there in the savanna for awhile.

Still, it's really not so disappointing to slip out of the reverie to discover that you are actually daydreaming in a faux-leopard-covered chair in the Explorer's Club at the Harbor Court Hotel. For this award-winning hotel on Baltimore's picturesque Inner Harbor lets one enjoy the thrill of a safari camp without so

much as sleeping in a tent. Instead, guests sojourn to rooms appointed in European-style elegance, as though housed in a grand English country manor.

Within the Explorer's Club, armchair adventurers can view Wullbrandt's wildlife mural, as well as another, reminiscent of 19th-century Italian paintings. Henredon game tables, wicker chairs, Chinese ginger jars, architectural engravings, high-quality antiques and even lamps with jutting tusks add to the "Out of Africa" mystique.

But this walk on the wild side has been conjured up in Maryland rather than the Dark Continent. David Murdock's

ᘓᘓ

HARBOR COURT HOTEL

550 LIGHT STREET

BALTIMORE, MD

(410) 234-0550

luxury hotel and lounge reflect both the renewed restoration of Baltimore's harbor area as well as his personal love of English and Oriental antiques. And he invests that passion abundantly in the decor of the lounge area.

Some trendy explorers have ventured in to relax in the exotic bar, prompting *InStyle* magazine to dub it a true hot spot: "…in the style of an English explorer's country home, decked out with a safari mural, ostrich-eggshell lamps and a tortoiseshell table. It attracts the likes of Bruce Willis, Holly Hunter, Jodie Foster, Nicolas Cage, Sharon Stone and, of course, Oriole shortstop Cal Ripken Jr."

In fact, the Harbor Court Hotel gets a lion's share of such attention. The hotel was featured in *Architectural Digest* while the Explorer's Club was dubbed "Baltimore's Best Piano Bar" by *Baltimore Magazine* for its nightly piano entertainment and weekend jazz. And *Condé Nast Traveler* judged it as the country's 11th best hotel, and its Hampton's restaurant as No. 2 in the nation.

But why take their word for it?

Venture into the Explorer's Club, nestling into the turn-of-the-century setting with your favorite martini, and let yourself be whisked to lands far, far away. If you close your eyes, you may even hear the distant chatter of monkeys and the trumpeting of elephants crossing the African plains…or at least strains of soothing piano music.

The Garden Court

*W*HETHER YOU'RE INCLINED to take high tea, engage in a light meal or linger over a favorite cocktail, the light and airy atrium of The Garden Court at Seattle's Four Seasons Olympic Hotel creates an inviting setting.

While the Italian Renaissance hotel's palatial lobby and luxurious Georgian Room restaurant are the peak of poshness, The Garden Court affords a more casual elegance, boasting cathe-

ಬಿಲ

FOUR SEASONS OLYMPIC HOTEL

411 UNIVERSITY STREET

SEATTLE, WA

(206) 621-1700

dral skylighted ceilings, palladium windows and an indoor forest of full-size trees.

Perhaps most notable, however, is the magnificent marble bar ensconced in The Garden Court that is famous for its prize-winning martinis.

Pull up a stool and order a *Cardinal Sin* that's loaded with Cherry Heering Liqueur, Kahlua, vintage port, brandy and vodka.

Or for a concoction with a true Pacific Northwest flavor, sip a *Rainier Martini* with Washington State Rainier Cherry infused with vodka. There's also the *Glacier Blue*, the *Olympic Gold* and the *Copper Illusion*.

The Garden Court also serves of a tasty selection of Northwestern cuisine and hors d'oeuvres to complement its popular martini menu.

On the weekends, live music and dancing as well as a Sunday buffet brunch are major drawing cards.

Harry Denton's Starlight Room

HARRY DENTON is known in San Francisco as "the man who views life as one big party." So if Harry is the host, then you can bet it will be an extravagant bash—one presented in elegant and opulent style.

Understandably, when the new owner of the Sir Francis Drake Hotel endeavored to breathe new life into the rooftop lounge a couple of years ago, he tapped Denton as the grand host.

Atop the historic 1928 landmark hotel, Harry Denton's Starlight Room exudes 1930s style and dress-up party savoir faire. The room itself is dressed up in luxurious furnishings that include crystal chandeliers, high-back velvet booth seating, a stand-up Biedermeier-style bar of black granite and blond burl, and voluptuous silk drapery.

Of course, its 360-degree view of downtown San Francisco and the hills beyond makes this an ideal leisure and cocktail respite, no matter how phenomenally the windows and room are adorned.

The stunningly glamorous 21st-story penthouse nightclub wrapped in glass is an altar to bon vivant Denton's over-the-top grandeur as a master of mood and detail.

The dance floor

๖ඏ

SIR FRANCIS DRAKE HOTEL

450 POWELL STREET

SAN FRANCISCO, CA

(415) 395-8595

Host Harry Denton

"It's like my dream living room," says Denton. "It's all about glamour...the perfect place to dance, drink and have fun. I just love it!"

This living room is filled with hundreds of yards of gold and burgundy silk, an ornate Axminster carpet from London, nine chandeliers, beveled mirror French doors and linen-damask-covered walls.

With all the glitz, a polished parquet dance floor and the swinging sounds of the Starlight Room Orchestra, those who want to trip the light fantastic couldn't ask for a more romantic venue. Denton has placed the dance floor right in front of the largest windows with their twinkling views of the city of lights, allowing the Fred and Ginger in all of us to swing in the starlight.

Of course, you don't have to dance. Simply slip into one of the plush mohair-tuxedo-upholstered booths and savor one Harry's decadent dessert specialties, a dash of caviar or one of the house martinis.

Infusion Bar and Restaurant

LIFE IN THE CITY has only one lane; fast. Infused with deadlines and phone lines, hem lines and lunch lines, the day can become fraught with the kind of tensions worth putting on ice come quittin' time—which, among the San Francisco chic, means "martini time" at the new Infusion Bar and Restaurant.

Known as a bar with a restaurant, the feature attraction which entices the mostly young '90s-trendy crowd to this hot

555 SECOND STREET

SAN FRANCISCO, CA

(415) 543-2282

spot is the multifarious selection of fresh fruit-infused vodkas shaken or stirred and served in an ice-cold martini glass. Tensions dissolve, conflicts cool and the socializing heats up

as celebrants gather around the hand-crafted wood bar for refreshing libations and, Thursday through Saturday, live acoustic-based music including rock 'n' roll, jazz and blues—or an infusion of all three.

The decor is contemporary and unobtrusive, elegant, yet casual—just what the trendsetters ordered. The bar, which runs the length of the restaurant, dominates the

narrow room, flanked by simple pine-topped tables. Modern suspended lights and sconces set the mood; plank-wood floors and putty-green walls blend into the background of a setting whose main attraction is an imposing array of glass decanters and fresh produce.

Guests may even be inclined to sidle up to the bar to drink their dinner, though the equally chic "new American" menu created by Chef David Fickes plays more than a supporting role in this bar-restaurant doubleheader. The menu is laced with spicy appetizers that complement the flavored vodkas, including roasted mussels glistening with lemon and anise-infused vodka or cornmeal-dusted calamari served with a jalapeño aioli.

Using only Skyy vodka, Infusions are made with the best seasonal produce available, which includes a selection of up to 75 intoxicating combinations. The produce infuses the vodka to a greater or lesser degree depending on the fruit, vegetable or spice, but does not eclipse the kick of quality vodka. Imagine the sweet kiss of watermelon, or the relentless fire of jalapeño; the exotic perfume of mango or the clean, refreshing effects of cucumber.

Though Infusions can be served any way guests can conjure; ice cold and up, like a martini, is the popular call. They are also great on the rocks or with a favorite juice or soda. For those seeking refreshment a little less spectacular but equally sleek, Infusion features a dramatic selection of fine California wines, as well as draft and bottled beer.

Infusion received three stars in a review by the *San Francisco Chronicle*, which also named it as one of the top 100 restaurants in the Bay Area, having chosen Chef David Fickes as a "Rising Star of Bay Area Cuisine." On the national level, *Wine Spectator* featured Infusion as a noteworthy addition to the San Francisco Bay Area.

Johnny Love's

"Our special brand of CONTROLLED CHAOS *is to ensure
one thing; that everyone has fun. We want everyone —
no matter if it's someone stopping by for lunch,
happy hour, dinner, a night of dancing or an employee
after a full shift — leaving here saying,
'That was a great time; I can't wait to go back'."*

— JOHNNY "LOVE" METHENY

THIS CALIFORNIA-STYLE classic supper club has the
personality of its celebrity bartender and owner, Johnny "Love"
Metheny. It's the only way it would have worked. Since opening
in August 1992, Johnny Love's has achieved legendary status as
one of San Francisco's hottest nightspots, owing to the legendary status of Johnny Love.

Metheny's celebrity status grew largely out of his establishment at some of San Francisco's finest: Henry Africa's, Harry's,
the Fillmore Grill and The Blue Light, many of which owe
some of their own success to his charismatic personality—
as well as his tricks of the trade.

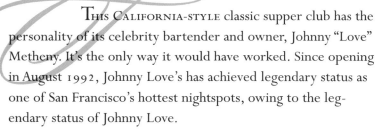

Johnny Love runs his own club on one signature premise:
Make sure guests have fun, which tends to incite many a walk
on the wild side. He has even been known to relinquish control
to certain of the rich and famous similarly inspired to try their
hand at pouring their own. Such novice bartenders have
included Bulls star Michael Jordan, Warriors basketball players,
Giants and A's baseball players, many of the 49ers, and British
billionaire Richard Branson.

The restaurant features "classic American cuisine," which,
to some, means hamburgers and fries, but to Johnny and his
followers, it suggests a creamy Caesar salad, scallop ceviche,

1500 BROADWAY

SAN FRANCISCO, CA

(415) 931-8021

ginger prawns or peppered monkfish. His calamari is nearly as famous as his charm.

Of course, with Stars veteran Mark "Spike" Hartman in the kitchen (Everyone has to have a name these days.), it's no wonder the food is worth writing home about. So start with a martini, save room for the cheesecake, and step out on the dance floor for some high-energy tunes including Motown, R&B, reggae and rock 'n' roll.

Johnny Love acquired his nickname while a University of California economics major, but he got past the advanced degree and capitalized on the name and his personality to become one of the city's most reputable bartenders and now, entrepreneur of a spot too hot for naught…

For those not quite ready for prime-time entertainment of the big city variety, Johnny Love has taken his party on the road, having opened two additional clubs in the suburbs of Walnut Creek and San Diego. They may not know what hit them, but they'll likely rise to the occasion just to see a guy named Johnny "Love" in action.

Johnny Love, left, and
Harry Denton

Le Colonial

SHUTTERED WINDOWS, period tiles, rattan furniture and swaying palm trees conjure up the magical image of French colonial Southeast Asia-Saigon, circa 1930. And the scents of Chef Gary Bau's savory and aromatic Vietnamese dishes wafting through the air from the dining area only fuel the time warp illusion.

But the magic here is no illusion. Le Colonial has introduced authentic Vietnamese flavor to West Hollywood and has done so with a style that mixes exotic elegance with a lived-in look.

Black-and-white photos of 1920s Vietnam under French rule line the staircase that leads up to the glamorous lounge, where wooden birdcages and Oriental rugs hearken to bygone days.

The South Seas outpost is a favorite haunt for a bevy of the rich and famous such as Sharon Stone, Hugh Grant, Susan Sarandon and other all-star players from trendy society and art and entertainment circles. But one need not be on any Who's Who list to enjoy the imported culinary treasures or cocktails under the pressed-tin ceiling of Le Colonial.

Both the first-floor restaurant and the upstairs lounge have drawing power. Some venture through the palm-lined entrance and into the chic plantation setting to relax under whirring ceiling fans and to savor Bau's grilled shrimp on sugar cane or steamed dumplings or perhaps just for dessert. Others head straight for the allure of Le Colonial's rich, shadowy lounge above where palms and bamboo mingle as naturally as the guests.

8783 BEVERLY BOULEVARD

WEST HOLLYWOOD, CA

(310) 289-0660

A few have even been known to slip out onto the veranda where good cigars and exotic cocktails transport them back to a balmy night in a paradise long forgotten.

The Lenox Room

THEY SAY THIS is the restaurant that's going to make it among a bevy of wannabe hot spots that have lined up like the young hopefuls in "A Chorus Line" along the Upper East Side of Manhattan. Most haven't made the cut. Contrary to the "old guard" of conservative affluent families that populate the neighborhood with generations of long-standing establishment, the turnover among local restaurants has been nothing short of relentless. Splendor can get boring.

But the Lenox Room just may have figured it out. Taking up residence along a precious slice of real estate known as Lenox Hill—they got the name right—executive chef and co-owner Charles Palmer, who continues to reign over his celebrated Aureole, and partner Tony Fortuna (Who could go wrong with a name like that?), a suave, amiable fellow who has managed a succession of Manhattan's finest, are both veterans of "the trend" and masters of the establishment.

The "Room," is a sleek-looking place, sort of a polo lounge, only subtler, with an understated decor of mirrors and tweedy banquettes. Attractive vases boasting a multitude of color are the only attention-seekers. It's part of the trend: The splash is in the service, the menu and the socialites. But then, the Lenox Room only looks a bit stuffy. It's an upscale neighborhood hangout for those who don't need to be seen, but might like to connect with good food and a good friend before heading home.

The food, like the atmosphere, isn't splashy, but it's all in very good taste. Spring rolls with lobster in a pool of that still-trendy cilantro sauce are a popular choice, as is the warm goat

1278 THIRD AVENUE

NEW YORK, NY

(212) 772-0404

cheese salad. Outrageous is saved for the warm carrot cheese-cake with rum raisin ice cream crowned with a poached pear and spiked with bittersweet chocolate. Heady is the wine list and its price list; though the sommelier, who has a voice like Peter Lorre and full knowledge of the showcase wine library, can be an important part of the selection.

The cocktail lounge mixes trend with traditional via its old mahogany-style bar with an aluminum counter. The bar seats approximately 15 people, but caters to twice that on any given evening. It's surrounded by unobtrusive sofas and banquettes in soft hues, in which another couple of dozen city-goers and business folks enjoy retreating for drinks at the end of a busy day.

According to Manager Franz Stuhlpfarrer, the atmosphere is comfortable, relaxed, and decidedly European across the front of the establishment, which opens up to the street like a French café. The result is an open, outdoor feeling from which lively music and conversation flow like wine. On Friday nights, the Lenox Room has become known for its "Martini Night," which has become the standard for regulars and those lucky enough to be in the right place at the right time. Cocktails are "reasonably priced," complimentary hors d'oeuvres are provided, and martinis reign supreme.

For the Lenox Room, the staying power just may be in the juxtaposition of an elegant restaurant with a hip bar and lounge area, which most guests prefer to combine into an entire evening experience.

The Mandarin Restaurant

GHIRARDELLI SQUARE is not just about chocolate. For nearly 30 years, The Mandarin Restaurant has been a mainstay at the square and a favorite place for Fisherman's Wharf sightseers as well as locals to congregate.

Good Chinese food is always a people magnet, but current owners decided to breathe new life into the once-neglected cocktail lounge with a plethoric slate of exotic and heady concoctions.

The bar prides itself on its *Mandarin Mai Tai* and swears that one will simply not be enough. Eastern-themed drinks come with vodka or rum and with seductive names such as *Mandarin Lady*, *Empress Delight*, *Concubine*, *Firecracker* and *Madarin Madness*. For the more daring, the *Dragon Fly*, *Philosopher* and the *Jade Dragon* are made with Chinese spirits.

And to keep pace with the times, The Mandarin has created three flavored martinis—the *Blue Sapphire*, *Red Gin-Gin* and *Melon-Collie*. The *Blue Sapphire* is a more traditional martini, while *Red Gin-Gin* has a sweet kick to it. The *Melon-Collie* is light and refreshing, but might leave a traditional martini lover feeling *pun*-ished as the name implies.

No matter what you're sipping, The Mandarin is a charming hideaway tucked amid burgundy brick walls with a candlelight ambiance.

Here, soft music soothes, exotic cocktails bewitch and the panoramic view of the bay reminds us of the importance of life's simple pleasures.

900 NORTH POINT

GHIRARDELLI SQUARE

SAN FRANCISCO, CA

(415) 673-8812

The Martini Club

WITHOUT A DOUBT, The Martini Club is the martini mecca of The South. Amid sleek art deco wrappings in a converted two-story 1920s Midtown home, the club's drink menu reads more like a Baskin Robbins slate of flavors (count 'em, 54!) than a trendy hipster hangout.

But whether you're a tried-and-true martini connoisseur in search of a *Classic* or a *Dirty* one or a cocktail gadabout willing to venture into martini decadence with a *Lady Godiva* or a *Georgia Peach*, you'll find liquid pleasure here in the shape of giant, chilled martini glasses.

Wander through the eight cozy, but colorful rooms—painted in Crayola-like hues of vibrant blue, red, aqua, olive and purple—to people watch or settle into plush oversize chairs or sink into one of the velvet-covered couches.

Designer side dishes include antiques, art deco lamps, posters and ashtrays. Fireplaces fuel extra coziness while a romantic outdoor patio attracts those wanting to escape the indoor buzz and revelry.

On the second floor, a cigar kiosk beckons puffers while a jazz pianist entertains nightly.

The club draws an eclectic clientele ranging from the Generation X crowd starring in their own version of "Casablanca" as they bite off the tips of their cigars with vigor to corporate execs wooing clients or escaping them after a long day. Sports and Hollywood celebrities are known to stop by to clip a tip and sip, too.

1140 CRESCENT AVENUE

ATLANTA, GA

(404) 873-0794

Its charm and character have earned The Martini Club nods from *Newsweek, The Atlanta Journal-Constitution* and *Vogue* as one of "Hotlanta's" top watering holes.

In fact, another of the bar's popular martinis sums up the joint's appeal quite simply. It's *Absolutely Fabulous.*

Mumbo Jumbo

LOOKING FOR a sexy, sizzling supper club to add a little heat to your night? Well, Mumbo Jumbo is a guaranteed hot spot.

Whether you want to sit down to a spicy meal in the way of award-winning consulting chef Guenter Seeger in the dramatic dining room or imbibe in the expansive bar and lounge area with a "Barcelona after dark" ambiance, you will feel the magic as soon as you enter this upscale "bar and grill." It's funky, artsy, contemporary and oh so swank.

89 PARK PLACE

ATLANTA, GA

(404) 523-0330

Co-owner Michael Krohngold describes the intriguing decor as "New Orleans, Memphis, Versace, Beetlejuice and voodoo, all thrown in a big pot."

No matter what the brew, the spell works.

Mosey on up to the bar in the 6,000-square-foot complex and you could be moseying for awhile since Mumbo Jumbo's 50-foot mahogany bar is thought to be the longest (and oldest) in Atlanta.

This trendy way station is hardly subtle. The building is swathed in velvet and a multitude of twinkling lights announce its name.

The dining room

The palatial dining room is decked out with columns adorned with white tile mosaics and bird- and flower-shaped lintels as well as a good deal of Gothic overtones. Crushed silk curtains, old brick with monkey frescoes, a fireplace salvaged from a former mayor's home and leatherback chairs add to the theatrical charm.

The long bar is illuminated with one-of-a-kind quirky vine-like lamps.

Large paintings over the bar, called prophet boxes, were created by artist Frank Hyder. When closed, they depict another image on the back.

After hours, the supper club evolves into a late-night lounge with DJ's and dancing and plenty of loud music.

But Mumbo Jumbo has a built-in escape for those seeking a more serene experience, and we don't mean the crawl space under the stairway rumored to have been a secret passage once used by Al Capone.

Rather, the cozy upstairs lounge, with its quiet men's study ambiance and leather sofas and easy chairs, invites premium sipping and cigar toking.

Mumbo Jumbo, which replaced the equally chic Velvet club, opened its revamped doors just a week before the Olympics invaded Atlanta. The club was soon a regular item in *The Atlanta Journal-Constitution's* PeachBuzz column with special events and celebrity sightings.

More than a year later, Mumbo Jumbo is still going for the gold…and getting it.

The longest bar in Atlanta

The view from outside

Pravda

I HAD HEARD it was there; set out the next evening. Took a ration of water, a co-pilot and a map, plenty of cash and a thirst for vodka. It wasn't there. Or maybe it was, but I wasn't. Maybe I was trying too hard. The secret to getting to Pravda is knowing you're already there.

Even if you know the whereabouts of Pravda, you could easily stroll right by the street lamp painted with Cyrillic letters that marks the obscure entrance to this cool basement nightspot on the edge of Soho.

But once inside—that is *if* you manage to make it through the club's selective door policy—it's not likely a place you'll soon forget. The decor is Bolshevik-inspired right down to hammer-and-sickle communist murals hearkening to the Russia of days gone by.

While the former cellar digs with honey-colored walls and thick archways might suggest proletariat, the crowd that swarms in for the caviar and vodka is definitely urban bourgeoisie.

They nibble caviar-laced potato chips and smoked fish, puff European smokes and lounge in overstuffed leather chairs. And they drink…for it is the beverage lineup that has people venturing underground in Manhattan. The house raspberry vodka is a favorite among the more than 70 different vodkas featured on the seven-page drink menu.

Cocktails are served by exotic beauties in little black dresses, who are careful to warn customers that the tops fall off the martini shakers delivered with the glasses. Believe them… unless you truly want a "splash" of vodka with your caviar.

281 LAFAYETTE STREET

NEW YORK, NY

(212) 226-4696

The limited food menu consists of caviar, zakouski (Russian hors d'oeuvres, some of which are served wrapped in Russian newsprint) and desserts. While it certainly isn't a full meal, it doesn't really matter. It's the seductive atmosphere that truly whets appetites for Pravda.

Notables who have ventured below for a vodka-and-caviar fling have included Mel Gibson, Robert DeNiro, Goldie Hawn and Ellen Barkin. The famous blondes even made tabloid headlines when they decided to dance on the bar.

Still not sure that an elusive, Soviet-inspired vodka bar can be truly hip? The truth is—after all, Pravda means "truth"—that if you can manage to get into the place, the beluga and cocktails will make you a loyal comrade.

The Rainbow Room

SUSPENDED AMONG THE STARS and the lights of the city, The Rainbow Room soars 65 stories above the heart of midtown Manhattan. The formal supper club made its debut in 1934 as the crowning jewel of Rockefeller Center, designed to be a social hub for the influential elite of New York to meet over cocktails and elegant cuisine and to dance to the beat of big bands on a revolving dance floor bathed in a rainbow of lights.

It received its colorful moniker in honor of a pipe organ that converted sounds into different hues and flooded the ceiling in a kaleidoscopic light show. The organ is long gone and a $20 million renovation was implemented in the '80s, but the dance floor still turns beneath the original crystal chandelier.

The Rainbow Room's art deco styling is enhanced by 24 floor-to-ceiling windows—each two stories high—that open onto dazzling wrap-around views of New York's famous skyline, rivers and bridges.

From the beginning, John D. Rockefeller envisioned The Rainbow Room as a world-renowned entertainment restaurant. His vision, gift-wrapped in glamour, has withstood the test of time, having achieved legendary status in a city known for trends and fads.

Today, music still harmonizes with glamour and gourmet cuisine and, of course, a rainbow of cocktails.

30 ROCKEFELLER PLAZA
NEW YORK, N.Y.
(212) 632-5000

Mixologist
Dale DeGroff

The Promenade Bar in The Rainbow Room is a perennial hot spot for Big Apple tipplers. Key reasons are the view and mixologist Dale DeGroff. The back bar boasts a stunning view that includes the Empire State Building, the World Trade Center and the Statue of Liberty, sentry of New York Harbor. Sunsets here are as intoxicating as the cocktails.

Guests may recognize the Promenade Bar from their favorite movies, including "Sleepless in Seattle." Film stars and other celebrities have always frequented The Rainbow Room. In decades past, one might have spotted Edgar Bergen, Mary Martin or Ella Fitzgerald, while more recent sightings have included "Lois and Clarke" star Teri Hatcher, actor Nicolas Cage and Aerosmith's Steven Tyler.

DeGroff, the man serving up libations, is a local celebrity of sorts himself, having earned the reputation as one of New York's friendliest bartenders and as "the da Vinci of drink." He's a collector of vintage cocktail recipe books and Prohibition literature; revival cocktails are his specialty. Plus if you can dream up a drink, this 20-year veteran cocktail Merlin can likely whip it up.

He's also known for conjuring up his own cocktail recipes as well as championing the classics, including tributes to yesteryear such as Chasen's vintage *Flame of Love Martini*, once available at that glamorous Hollywood haunt. While a Miami Beach bartender is credited with inventing the *Cosmopolitan*, many connoisseurs would concur that DeGroff has perfected it.

DeGroff is a martini drinker, preferring a classic dry one with an olive and a twist.

"The twist was the first martini garnish…before olives," explains DeGroff, who rattles off cocktail history and trivia faster than you can shake a martini. But this bartender doesn't shake his martinis, Mr. Bond.

"There is such a thing as *bruising* the gin, but it doesn't actually harm anything. It's basically that shaking any liquid changes the texture by putting millions of air bubbles into it. I love that heavy, cold, silky sensation of a stirred martini."

He also contends there's no such thing as a *true* martini without vermouth. "It's amazing that there are only two ingredients to a traditional martini and yet they each bring a lot to the drink." While vodka has now replaced gin in many martini recipes, the veteran mixer considers vodka a bit of an enigma.

"But the gin martini is not the end all and be all of cocktails. I don't mind the martini name being applied to all sorts of new drinks. I'm not going to become the Ronald Reagan of the cocktail."

He has watched the martini evolve through the year and encourages young bartenders to take their skill levels beyond being "shot and beer" guys. He loves to see creativity behind the bar. The designer martini keeps popping up in new forms and yet still maintains its status as the "king of cocktails."

Of course, that moniker could apply to DeGroff, himself.

Ritz-Carlton Bar

"I never should have switched from scotch to martinis..."

— HUMPHREY BOGART

FROM THE MOMENT Cesar Ritz opened the Hotel Ritz of Paris in 1898, to the 1910 debut of The Ritz-Carlton Hotels in the United States, he set the standard of providing guests with the finest locations and superior cuisine, beverages and furnishings, as well as a professional, dedicated staff.

The 87-year old Nob Hill landmark building, once hailed as the "temple of commerce" when it opened in 1909, re-opened in April 1991 as the Ritz-Carlton San Francisco—a 336-room luxury hotel, crafted and presented with the cornerstone standards of excellence in service and unparalleled elegance established by its founder nearly 100 years before.

The Ritz-Carlton San Francisco

The hotel's interior is decorated with 18th- and 19th-century antiques and artwork that complement the historic Neo-classical exterior. Furnishings and fabrics were selected not only for comfort and beauty, but also to respect the architecture's history and recognize San Francisco as a crossroads to the world.

Since its establishment in the United States, the Ritz-Carlton has become the home away from home for politicians,

600 STOCKTON STREET

SAN FRANCISCO, CA

(415) 296-7465

kings and queens, Hollywood personalities, playwrights and
newsmakers around the world.

The Scotch Bar

Thus, it is certainly no surprise that a guest would be availed of the most refined libations at San Francisco's Ritz-Carlton Bar, including the country's largest selection of the world's finest single malt scotches.

The scotch collection encompasses 125 distilleries and represents Scotland's finest lowland, highland and island whiskeys, ranging from Macallan and Springbank to Bowmore. Young whiskeys include Auchentoshan, Cragganmore and Laphroaig.

Single malt scotch is defined by very specific criterion: The only raw ingredient, malted barley, is smoked over peat fires, mixed with water, fermented, distilled and traditionally aged in oak barrels. It is created in just one distillery and must be made in Scotland.

True scotch aficionados report that no two brands of single malt scotch—and no two bottles of the same brand—are alike. The subtleties in a glass of malt scotch rival those in a glass of fine wine. Elements of aroma, body and finish are distinguishing characteristics, making "nosing" a common practice for tastings.

The Ritz-Carlton Bar offers a relaxed, intimate setting in which to "nose" single malt scotches. The bar also offers a wide assortment of fine Cuban cigars; a right-hand complement to a glass of fine scotch.

Of course, if scotch isn't your "fashion," the Ritz pours an exceptional martini. I suspect Bogey would have been pleased either way.

San Ysidro Ranch

Nestled between the Santa Ynez Mountains and the Pacific on 540 tranquil acres, San Ysidro Ranch is known for just about every amenity a guest might possibly desire when expecting to be indulged. So, go ahead, expect a good martini, too.

Sequestered in the foothills of Montecito, California, the Ranch has served as a luxurious retreat and place of respite for more than 100 years. Its privacy sought by Hollywood and political figures through the decades, such as John Husten, Gloria Swanson, Merle Oberon, David Niven, Vivien Leigh, Sir Lawrence Olivier, William Powell, Jean Harlow, Richard Nixon, Hubert Humphrey, Adlai Stevenson and the Kennedys.

The tranquillity that inspired poets and writers the likes of Sinclair Lewis, and the simple pleasures of horseback riding, scenic strolls and restorative "body work" including plein aire massage, spa treatments and whirlpool baths are still engaging the known and unknown, distinguished and undistinguished guests at San Ysidro Ranch.

The ranch is named for Saint Isadore (San Ysidro in Spanish), an impoverished man who was born in Madrid in 1070 and passed away 60 years later, but only after a life of service to the hungry, the poor and the destitute. For this effort, the Catholic Church canonized him in 1622.

Legend has it that the reverent Ysidro was given to attend regular Mass, a practice that angered his fellow field workers, as it cut into his work time. Yet, when the foreman came to mitigate the transgression, he witnessed a team of snow-white oxen laboring beside Ysidro and his own team, enabling him to complete his tasks on time.

900 San Ysidro Lane

Santa Barbara, CA

(805) 969-5046

Thus, San Ysidro, who become the patron saint of farmers, is always depicted surrounded by a plow, a team of oxen and an angel.

The ranch's Stonehouse Restaurant, renowned for the fresh produce and other natural ingredients commanded by Chef Gerhard Thompson in the preparation of his classically "American cuisine," was once called the Plow and Angel; a name now given to the lively pub originally built in 1893 as the ranch wine cellar.

The Plow and Angel Pub pours generous libations nightly alongside hearty food selections, served in casual, relaxing surroundings.

The oak bar built in the days of Colman and Weingand still dominates the former cellar. A 1958 Wurlitzer jukebox provides unlimited free play of classic tunes whenever live jazz is not on tap.

Leather couches and intimate corners invite romance and stimulating conversation amid century-old sandstone walls covered with vintage photographs detailing the ranch's rich history.

Tongue & Groove

TAKING A CUE from Parisian cafés and South Beach bistros, Tongue & Groove can't help but be hip. Of course, that was the intention all along—to convert a stark white, sterile left-over-from-the-'80s look into a bright, colorful haven with a cartoonish spirit that would appeal to Baby Boomers and Generation X'ers alike.

Its funky flair and delectable fare have earned Tongue & Groove accolades and fans galore. For *Atlanta* magazine's Best

of Atlanta 1995 honors, the cocktail lounge was named the Southern metropolis' Best Nightspot. It was back on the winner's list again in 1996 as Best Bar for Schmoozing.

Here you schmooze and sip libations in rooms with wood floors, undulating walls and animated furnish-

3055 PEACHTREE ROAD N.E.

ATLANTA, GA

(404) 261-2325

ings—including custom artistic contributions such as the tile mosaic entrance, painted murals, mixed-media creations and photographs of femmes fatale de nuit on the dance floor.

Not only can you sample a *Nutini* or a *Sky Blue* from the martini menu, but you can also nibble on sushi or paté while unwinding to the night's music mix. This visual masterpiece of a bar celebrates the resurgence of listening music mixed with dance music.

Whether the name dictates the atmosphere or the atmosphere inspired the name, it works. The "tongue" is vital to conversation and tasting both culinary and cocktail creations while clubgoers can get in the "groove" on any number of musical themed nights—from Latin dance tunes to acid jazz to the retro "Saturday Night Fever" sounds of the '70s.

Tongue & Groove is a place to see and be seen for business men and women, curious tourists, a mellow mix of aging hipsters, night owls, artistic types and loyal locals. Plus, the bar itself is a "you-gotta-see-this-place" kind of attraction.

Attitude and aesthetics add up to stylized sophistication. And in this case they add up to Tongue & Groove.

Top of the Hub

WHAT MAKES the Top of the Hub a landmark would likely be the landmark building in which it makes its home, and which recently received a $4 million renovation, except that many look beyond the building to the "widest, highest, most impressive" panoramic view of Boston ever seen, from the 52nd floor of the Prudential Tower.

The Skywalk View and Exhibit at the Top of the Hub restaurant enable visitors to discover Boston at a glance, while enjoying a show of some of the country's renowned artists such as Cynthia Thompson, Barbara Sebastian and Karl Umlauf; as well as creative displays inspired by people and events of historical proportion.

In "Faces Wall," an exhibit of portraits of the men and women who crafted the heritage of Boston, an image of Anne Sexton reveals the poem she wrote titled, "Just Once." Behind a picture of Red Auerbach is the brand of cigar for which he was known and beside Copley's famous portrait of Sam Adams is a bottle of his namesake beer.

The "new and renewed" restaurant features American cuisine with a characteristic focus on fresh seafood. Executive Chef Dean Moore capitalizes on the catch of the day and freshest ingredients in the famous Boston Market to create consistently flavorful menus that encounter only seasonal changes. A few of his signature dishes include Maine crab meat spring rolls and Plymouth trout as well as medallions of veal and a grilled vegetable lasagna.

The new bar and lounge area serves as the centerpiece for the restaurant, creating a spacious, club-like ambiance with the appeal of a sophisticated exclusive...except that everyone feels

Top of the Hub
RESTAURANT & SKYWALK

PRUDENTIAL TOWER

800 BOYLSTON STREET

BOSTON, MA

(617) 536-1775

welcome. Verde marble tabletops are accented in bright chrome detail while warm, rich hues help reduce the glare of large window areas.

Here you can drink in the amazing view while you sip the bar's signature drink, *The Cosmopolitan*, served in a stemless martini glass cradled in a bowl of crushed ice.

At this point, Top of the Hub is considered a landmark of its own, in a landmark building, within a landmark town. Expect the experience to be, well...landmark.

The Viper Room

HOLLYWOOD has done a lot to foster the allure of martinis with perhaps James Bond and George Burns giving them an extra boost. Agent 007 is famous for giving directions on how he likes his dry martinis "shaken not stirred" and Burns

just plain enjoyed martinis. "Happiness is a dry martini and a good woman...or a bad woman," said the legendary comedian, who also professed, "I never go jogging, it makes me spill my martini."

Now Johnny Depp and his Viper Room partner Sal Jenco are enticing New Hollywood to grab a stem and swill any of eleven custom martinis featured at Mr. Phat's Royal Martini Club in The Viper Room each Thursday night.

Since its 1993 debut, The Viper Room has played host to the likes of Bruce Springsteen, Sheryl Crow, Dennis Rodman, Counting Crows, Lenny Kravitz, Johnny Cash, Sandra Bernhardt and Tom Petty and the Heartbreakers, as well as cult favorites of America's underground.

The intimate nightclub is reminiscent of Harlem's great jazz clubs of the 1920s. Granted, the place is small—holding only 250 people—but that's the attraction when big name entertainers take to the stage, almost rubbing elbows with the fans. It's become The Viper Room's trademark, along with surprise appearances on any given night.

Mr. Phat's Royal Martini Club is also a club trademark, hosted by Dean R. Miller, "The Sultan of Swing." This weekly event showcases live performances of big band, swing, rocka-

∞

8852 SUNSET BOULEVARD

WEST HOLLYWOOD, CA

(310) 358-1881

billy, blues and jazz sounds. Guest artists range from Brian Setzer and his orchestra to the legendary "Queen of Boogie Woogie," Hadda Brooks.

The Martini Club serves up an assortment of top-shelf concoctions from its calling-card menu. Cigar smokers are welcome here and patrons are encouraged to don cocktail attire for this choice evening, "where cocktails are king and the music is swing!"

The Viper Room clearly caters to a broad range of tastes, whether you like to swig and swing to Pearl Jam or Royal Crown Revue. So swing on…

The bar at Infusion

Martini
Recipes

All Too Important Martini

JOHNNY LOVE'S
SAN FRANCISCO

Touch of dry vermouth (one part to 8 parts Tanqueray Gin)
2½ oz. Tanqueray Gin
2 olives for garnish

Pour vermouth into a chilled glass and swirl it around. Dump the vermouth into the sink. Chill the Tanqueray Gin until cold and strain into the glass. Garnish with the two olives skewered on a pick.

TRADE SECRET

What goes into making a perfect martini is a question that will be argued as long as drinkers exist. First, you don't shake a martini, you stir a martini. Also, the glass must be chilled. The best martini is made when you pour the gin while looking at the bottle of vermouth.

Blue Sapphire

THE MANDARIN
SAN FRANCISCO

Splash of dry vermouth
3 oz. Bombay Sapphire Gin
1 oz. Blue Curaçao
1 cherry for garnish

Stir with ice and strain into a chilled martini glass. Garnish with the cherry.

Classic Dry

THE MARTINI CLUB
ATLANTA, GEORGIA

2½ oz. Bombay Gin
   Splash of vermouth
1 lemon twist for garnish

Stir with ice and strain into a chilled martini glass. Garnish with the lemon twist.

Classic Extra Dry

THE MARTINI CLUB
ATLANTA, GEORGIA

2½ oz. Bombay Sapphire Gin
   1 lemon twist for garnish

Stir with ice and strain into a chilled martini glass. Garnish with the lemon twist.

Classic Old Fashioned Martini

THE LENOX ROOM
NEW YORK CITY

3 oz. Boodles Gin
1 oz. Noilly Prat Vermouth Sec

Stir with ice and pour into a chilled martini glass.

Classic Sapphire

THE COVEY
CARMEL, CALIFORNIA

2 oz. Bombay Sapphire Gin
2 drops dry vermouth
1 olive for garnish

Fill shaker with ice. Add gin and vermouth. Shake or stir until well chilled. Strain into a martini glass. Garnish with the olive.

Copper Illusion

**GARDEN COURT
AT THE FOUR SEASONS
OLYMPIC HOTEL**
SEATTLE, WASHINGTON

¼ oz. Cointreau liqueur
¼ oz. Campari
1½ oz. Beefeater Gin
1 orange twist for garnish

Spoon-twirl 40 revolutions with ice and strain into a chilled martini glass. Garnish with the orange twist.

Dirty Gin Martini

JOHNNY LOVE'S
SAN FRANCISCO

Touch of dry vermouth
2½ oz. Tanqueray Gin
Splash of olive juice
2 olives for garnish

Pour vermouth into a chilled glass and swirl it around. Dump the vermouth into the sink. Chill the Tanqueray Gin until cold and strain into the glass. Pour in a splash of olive juice and garnish with the two olives skewered on a pick.

Gibson Martini

JOHNNY LOVE'S
SAN FRANCISCO

Touch of dry vermouth
2½ oz. Tanqueray Gin
1 onion for garnish

Pour vermouth into a chilled glass and swirl it around. Dump the vermouth into the sink. Chill the Tanqueray Gin until cold and strain into the glass. Garnish with the onion.

Harry's Martini

HARRY DENTON'S
STARLIGHT ROOM
SAN FRANCISCO

2 oz. Bombay Gin
¼ oz. green chartreuse
1 lemon twist for garnish

Shake with ice and strain into a chilled martini glass. Garnish with the lemon twist.

Knickerbocker Martini

THE RAINBOW ROOM
NEW YORK CITY

1½ oz. dry gin
1½ oz. French dry vermouth
2 dashes orange bitters
Lemon peel for garnish

Stir with ice and strain into a chilled martini glass. Garnish with the lemon peel.

Martinez

THE RAINBOW ROOM
NEW YORK CITY

1 lemon wedge
2 oz. Old Tom Gin
1 oz. Italian sweet vermouth
½ oz. Maraschino liqueur
2 dashes simple syrup
2 dashes Angostura bitters

Squeeze the lemon wedge into a chilled martini glass and leave the wedge for garnish. Shake other ingredients with ice. Strain into the martini glass.

Night Shift Martini

CLUB 36
SAN FRANCISCO

2½ oz. Bombay Sapphire Gin
Splash of Galliano
1 olive for garnish

Stir with ice and strain into a chilled martini glass. Garnish with the olive.

Parisian Martini

COMPASS ROSE
SAN FRANCISCO

2½ oz. Tanqueray Gin
Dash of Pernod
1 Tom olive for garnish

Stir with ice and strain into a chilled martini glass. Garnish with the Tom olive.

Park Avenue

JOHNNY LOVE'S

SAN FRANCISCO

2½ oz. Tanqueray Gin
1 oz. pineapple juice
Splash of vermouth

Combine with ice and shake. Strain into a chilled martini glass.

Park Place Martini

MUMBO JUMBO

ATLANTA, GEORGIA

1 oz. Bombay Sapphire Gin
1 oz. Chambord raspberry liqueur
Dash of Triple Sec
1 lemon zest for garnish

Shake with ice and strain into a chilled martini glass. Garnish with the lemon zest.

Perfect Martini

JOHNNY LOVE'S

SAN FRANCISCO

Touch of dry vermouth
Touch of sweet vermouth
2½ oz. Tanqueray Gin
2 olives for garnish

Pour vermouths into a chilled glass and swirl them around. Dump the vermouths into the sink. Chill the Tanqueray Gin until cold and strain into the glass. Garnish with the two olives skewered on a pick.

Pure Martini

**THE RITZ-CARLTON BAR
AT THE RITZ-CARLTON**

SAN FRANCISCO

2 oz. Bombay Sapphire Gin
1 tsp. Noilly Prat Dry Vermouth
2 Spanish cocktail olives for garnish

In a shaker half-filled with ice, combine gin and vermouth. Shake well, 10 to 12 shakes, and strain into a chilled martini glass. Garnish with the olives skewered on a pick.

Red Gin-Gin

THE MANDARIN

SAN FRANCISCO

Dry vermouth
3 oz. gin
1 oz. sloe gin
1 spiral orange twist for garnish

Stir with ice and strain into a chilled martini glass. Garnish with the spiral orange twist.

Supper Martini

MUMBO JUMBO

ATLANTA, GEORGIA

2 oz. Boodles Gin
Dash of Drambuie
Dash of sweet vermouth
1 cherry for garnish

Shake with ice and strain into a chilled martini glass. Garnish with the cherry.

Thin Man Martini

THE RAINBOW ROOM
NEW YORK CITY

3 oz. dry gin
1 oz. French dry vermouth
Olive for garnish

Stir ingredients with ice to chill and strain into a chilled martini glass. Garnish with the olive.

Yang Martini

INAGIKU
NEW YORK CITY

2½ oz. gin
½ oz. sake

Stir with ice and strain into a chilled martini glass.

Ying Martini

INAGIKU
NEW YORK CITY

2½ oz. sake
½ oz. gin

Stir with ice and strain into a chilled martini glass.

Absolut Sensation

COMPASS ROSE
SAN FRANCISCO

2½ oz. Absolut Vodka
    Splash of Chambord raspberry liqueur
1 raspberry for garnish

Stir with ice and strain into a chilled martini glass. Garnish with the raspberry.

Absolutly Fabulous

THE MARTINI CLUB
ATLANTA, GEORGIA

1¼ oz. Absolut Citron Vodka
1¼ oz. Absolut Kurant Vodka
   1 lemon twist for garnish

Stir with ice and strain into a chilled martini glass. Garnish with the lemon twist.

Antini

**HARRY DENTON'S
STARLIGHT ROOM**
SAN FRANCISCO

2 oz. Stolichnaya Cristall Vodka
½ oz. Lillet Rouge*
  1 burnt orange twist for garnish

Shake with ice and strain into a chilled martini glass. Garnish with the burnt orange twist.

Lillet Rouge is a French apéritif made from a blend of red wine, brandy, fruits and herbs.

Blue Skyy Martini

COMPASS ROSE

SAN FRANCISCO

2½ oz. Skyy Vodka
   Splash of Blue Curaçao

Stir with ice and strain into a chilled martini glass.

Cajun Martini

COMPASS ROSE

SAN FRANCISCO

2½ oz. Absolut Peppar Vodka
   1 jalapeño pepper for garnish

Stir with ice and strain into a chilled martini glass. Garnish with the jalapeño pepper.

Campton Cosmo

CAMPTON PLACE HOTEL

SAN FRANCISCO

1½ oz. Absolut Citron Vodka
   ¾ oz. Tuaca
      Splash of cranberry juice
   ½ oz. lemon juice
   1 kumquat for garnish

Stir with ice and strain into a chilled martini glass. Garnish with the kumquat.

The Campton Cure by Campton Place Hotel

Campton Cure

CAMPTON PLACE HOTEL

SAN FRANCISCO

1 oz. Absolut Citron Vodka

½ oz. Cointreau

3 squeezes lime juice

Splash of cranberry juice

Stir with ice and strain into a chilled martini glass.

Cardinal Sin

**GARDEN COURT
AT THE FOUR SEASONS
OLYMPIC HOTEL**

SEATTLE, WASHINGTON

⅛ oz. Cherry Heering Liqueur*

⅛ oz. Kahlua

½ oz. Late Bottle Vintage Port, 1988 Fonseca

½ oz. Janneau Grand Armagnac Brandy

2 oz. Ketel One Vodka

1 orange twist, air dried, for garnish

Spoon-twirl or shake lightly with ice and strain into a chilled martini glass. Garnish with the orange twist.

Cherry Heering is a dark red, cherry-flavored liqueur from Denmark.

Champagne Royale de Martini

TONGUE & GROOVE

ATLANTA, GEORGIA

1½ oz. premium vodka

1 oz. Veuve Clicquot Yellow Label Champagne

½ oz. Chambord raspberry liqueur

1 lemon twist for garnish

Stir with ice and strain into a chilled martini glass. Garnish with the lemon twist.

Chesapeake Martini

EXPLORER'S CLUB

BALTIMORE, MARYLAND

2 oz. Stolichnaya Pepper Vodka

1 Tbsp. clam or oyster liquor

2 dashes Crystal Hot Sauce

½ tsp. Old Bay Seasoning

1 cherry tomato for garnish

1 fresh oyster for garnish

Combine first four ingredients over ice in a shaker. Strain into a chilled glass. Garnish with the skewered cherry tomato and freshly shucked oyster.

Chocolate Martini

JOHNNY LOVE'S

SAN FRANCISCO

2½ oz. Tanqueray Sterling Vodka

Splash of white crème de cacao

Pour ingredients into a shaker glass with ice. Stir and strain into a chilled martini glass.

Citrus Brandy Martini

PRAVDA

NEW YORK CITY

3 oz. Stolichnaya Limonnaya

¾ oz. Cointreau

¼ oz. lemon juice

Stir with ice and strain into a chilled martini glass.

Citrus Martini

COMPASS ROSE

SAN FRANCISCO

2½ oz. Absolut Citron Vodka

1 lemon zest for garnish

Stir with ice and strain into a chilled martini glass. Garnish with the lemon zest.

Contemporary

THE COVEY

CARMEL, CALIFORNIA

2 oz. Absolut Citron Vodka

4 drops Cointreau

1 orange peel for garnish

Fill shaker with ice. Add vodka and Cointreau. Shake until well chilled. Strain into a martini glass. Garnish with the orange peel.

The Cosmopolitan

TOP OF THE HUB

BOSTON, MASSACHUSETTS

2 oz. Stolichnaya Vodka

Splash of Triple Sec

Dash of Roses Lime Juice

Splash of cranberry juice

1 lime twist for garnish

3 craisins (dried cranberries) for garnish

Stir with ice and strain into a stemless martini glass that is cradled in a bowl of crushed ice. Garnish with the lime twist and craisins.

*The Cosmopolitan,
signature drink at
Top of the Hub*

Dark Crystal

COMPASS ROSE

SAN FRANCISCO

**2½ oz. Stolichnaya Cristall Vodka
Splash of Remy Martin VSOP
1 lemon twist for garnish**

Stir with ice and strain into a chilled martini glass. Garnish
with the lemon twist.

Diamond Martini

COMPASS ROSE
SAN FRANCISCO

2½ oz. Stolichnaya Cristall Vodka
1 Tom olive for garnish

Stir with ice and strain into a chilled martini glass. Garnish with the Tom olive.

Dirty Martini

THE MARTINI CLUB
ATLANTA, GEORGIA

2¼ oz. Ketel One Vodka
¼ oz. olive juice
3 olives for garnish

Stir with ice and strain into a chilled martini glass. Garnish with the olives skewered on a pick.

Dirty Vodka Martini

TONGUE & GROOVE
ATLANTA, GEORGIA

1½ oz. premium vodka
½ oz. olive juice
3 olives for garnish

Stir with ice and strain into a chilled martini glass. Garnish with the three olives skewered on a pick.

Dog Bites Back

THE MARTINI CLUB
ATLANTA, GEORGIA

1 oz. Skyy Vodka
1½ oz. Bloody Mary mix
2 Cajun olives for garnish
1 lemon twist for garnish

Stir with ice and strain into a chilled martini glass. Garnish with the olives and lemon twist.

Double White Chocolate Martini

MUMBO JUMBO
ATLANTA, GEORGIA

1¼ oz. Belvedere Vodka
½ oz. Godet*
¼ oz. white crème de cacao
1 chocolate swizzle stick for garnish

Shake with ice and strain into a chilled martini glass. Garnish with the chocolate swizzle stick.

* Godet is a white chocolate liqueur.

Dutch Martini

THE MARTINI CLUB
ATLANTA, GEORGIA

2½ oz. Ketel One Vodka
3 Tom olives for garnish

Stir with ice and strain into a chilled martini glass. Garnish with the olives skewered on a pick.

Framboise Martini

SAN YSIDRO RANCH

SANTA BARBARA,
CALIFORNIA

2 oz. Absolut Vodka

¼ oz. Chambord raspberry liqueur

1 raspberry for garnish

Pour ingredients into shaker with ice. Shake for 15 seconds and strain into a chilled martini glass. Garnish with the fresh raspberry.

Frangelico Martini

PRAVDA

NEW YORK CITY

3 oz. Absolut Vodka

¾ oz. Frangelico liqueur*

½ oz. Tuaca liqueur

Stir with ice and strain into a chilled martini glass.

Frangelico is a hazelnut-flavored liqueur enhanced with the essence of flowers and berries.

French Martini

PRAVDA

NEW YORK CITY

2½ oz. vodka

½ oz. Chambord raspberry liqueur

1 oz. pineapple juice

Stir with ice and strain into a chilled martini glass.

Fuzzy Martini

CLUB 36
SAN FRANCISCO

2½ oz. Stolichnaya Ohranj Vodka
Splash of peach schnapps

Stir with ice and strain into a chilled martini glass.

Georgia Peach

THE MARTINI CLUB
ATLANTA, GEORGIA

1 oz. Ketel One Vodka
½ oz. peach schnapps
1 oz. orange juice
1 peach slice for garnish

Stir with ice and strain into a chilled martini glass. Garnish with the peach slice.

Ginseng Martini

LE COLONIAL
WEST HOLLYWOOD,
CALIFORNIA

1 American ginseng root
1 bottle of vodka
Splash of dry vermouth
Ginger slice for garnish

Cure ginseng root in a bottle of vodka for 1 week. Pour 2 oz. of vodka over ice with a splash of dry vermouth. Shake and strain. Garnish with the slice of ginger.

Grand Martini

TONGUE & GROOVE

ATLANTA, GEORGIA

1 oz. premium vodka
½ oz. Grand Marnier
1 lemon twist for garnish

Stir with ice and strain into a chilled martini glass. Garnish with the lemon twist.

Grand Vodka Martini

THE MARTINI CLUB

ATLANTA, GEORGIA

2¼ oz. Ketel One Vodka
¼ oz. Grand Marnier
1 orange slice for garnish

Stir with ice and strain into a chilled martini glass. Garnish with the orange slice.

James Bond Martini

**RITZ-CARLTON BAR
AT THE RITZ-CARLTON**

SAN FRANCISCO

2 oz. Stolichnaya Vodka
½ tsp. Noilly Prat Vermouth
1 lemon twist for garnish

In a shaker half-filled with ice, combine vodka and vermouth. Shake very well and strain into a chilled martini glass. Peel lemon zest over martini and garnish with the lemon twist.

Infusion Bar and Restaurant

Kurant Chocolate Martini

CAMPTON PLACE HOTEL

SAN FRANCISCO

1 oz. Absolut Kurant Vodka
1 oz. Godiva chocolate liqueur
1 raspberry for garnish
1 coconut slice for garnish

Stir with ice and strain into a chilled martini glass. Garnish with the raspberry and coconut slice.

Kurant Cosmopolitan

COMPASS ROSE

SAN FRANCISCO

2½ oz. Absolut Kurant Vodka
Dash of Triple Sec
Splash of cranberry juice
Juice from 1 lime
1 lemon twist for garnish

Stir with ice and strain into a chilled martini glass. Garnish with the lemon twist.

Lady Godiva

THE MARTINI CLUB

ATLANTA, GEORGIA

Cocoa
2 oz. Smirnoff Vodka
½ oz. Godiva chocolate liqueur
¼ oz. white crème de cacao
1 Hershey's Kiss for garnish

Wet the rim of the chilled martini glass with water. Dip in cocoa and brush off any extra cocoa. Stir the vodka and liqueurs with ice. Strain carefully into the cocoa-rimmed martini glass. Garnish with the Hershey's Kiss.

Lemon Cosmopolitan

THE MARTINI CLUB
ATLANTA, GEORGIA

2 oz. Absolut Citron Vodka
½ oz. cranberry juice
　Splash of Triple Sec
　Splash of Sprite
1 lemon twist for garnish

Stir with ice and strain into a chilled martini glass. Garnish with the lemon twist.

Lemon Drop Martini

TONGUE & GROOVE
ATLANTA, GEORGIA

　Sugar
1½ oz. Absolut Citron Vodka
¼ oz. Triple Sec
¼ oz. sweet and sour mix

Wet the rim of the chilled martini glass with water. Dip in sugar and brush off any extra. Stir the vodka, Triple Sec and sweet and sour mix with ice. Strain carefully into the sugar-rimmed martini glass.

Lenox Room Peachy Keen Martini

THE LENOX ROOM
NEW YORK CITY

2 oz. vodka
1 tsp. peach purée
3 oz. peach nectar
　Peach slice for garnish

Stir with ice and strain into a chilled martini glass. Garnish with the peach slice.

Limonnaya Martini

THE MARTINI CLUB
ATLANTA, GEORGIA

White sugar
2¼ oz. Stolichnaya Vodka
¼ oz. sour mix

Wet the rim of the chilled martini glass with water. Dip in white sugar and brush off any extra sugar. Stir the vodka and sour mix with ice. Strain carefully into the sugar-rimmed martini glass.

Litchi Martini

LE COLONIAL
WEST HOLLYWOOD,
CALIFORNIA

1 oz. litchi juice
1¾ oz. vodka
2 litchi nuts for garnish

Pour over ice. Shake and serve in a chilled martini glass. Garnish with the litchi nuts skewered on a pick.

Melon Citrus Martini

PRAVDA
NEW YORK CITY

3 oz. Absolut Vodka
1 oz. Midori liqueur*
¼ oz. lime juice

Stir with ice and strain into a chilled martini glass.

Midori liqueur is a Japanese liqueur that has the flavor of honeydew melon.

Melon Martini

TONGUE & GROOVE
ATLANTA, GEORGIA

1½ oz. premium vodka
½ oz. Midori liqueur*
1 maraschino cherry for garnish

Stir with ice and strain into a chilled martini glass. Garnish with the maraschino cherry.

Midori liqueur is a Japanese liqueur that has the flavor of honeydew melon.

Melon Vodka Martini

COMPASS ROSE
SAN FRANCISCO

2½ oz. Absolut Vodka
Dash of Midori liqueur*
Fresh lime juice

Stir with ice and strain into a chilled martini glass.

Midori liqueur is a Japanese liqueur that has the flavor of honeydew melon.

Melon-Collie

THE MANDARIN
SAN FRANCISCO

Splash of dry vermouth
3 oz. vodka
1 oz. Midori liqueur*
1 spiral lemon twist for garnish

Stir with ice and strain into a chilled martini glass. Garnish with the spiral lemon twist.

Midori liqueur is a Japanese liqueur that has the flavor of honeydew melon.

Melontini

THE LENOX ROOM
NEW YORK CITY

2 oz. vodka
4 oz. watermelon juice
    Dash of Noilly Prat Vermouth Sec
    Watermelon for garnish

Stir with ice and strain into a chilled martini glass. Garnish with the watermelon wedge.

Mr. Phat's Citrus Martini

THE VIPER ROOM
WEST HOLLYWOOD,
CALIFORNIA

2½ oz. Absolut Citron Vodka
    1 lemon slice for garnish

Stir with ice and strain into a chilled martini glass. Garnish with the lemon slice.

Mumbo Martini

MUMBO JUMBO

ATLANTA, GEORGIA

2 oz. Russian Roulette Vodka
½ oz. olive juice
   Splash of dry vermouth
3 small martini olives for garnish
3 cocktail onions for garnish

Shake with ice and strain into a chilled martini glass. Garnish with the olives and onions skewered on picks.

Nutini

TONGUE & GROOVE

ATLANTA, GEORGIA

1½ oz. premium vodka
½ oz. Frangelico liqueur*

Stir with ice and strain into a chilled martini glass.

* Frangelico is a hazelnut-flavored liqueur enhanced with the essence of flowers and berries.

Ozzon Martini

CLUB 36

SAN FRANCISCO

2½ oz. Skyy Vodka
   Splash of Romana Sambuca
1 olive for garnish

Stir with ice and strain into a chilled martini glass. Garnish with the olive.

Patsy's Martini

THE MARTINI CLUB
ATLANTA, GEORGIA

1½ oz. Stolichnaya Vodka
1 oz. champagne

Stir with ice and strain into a chilled martini glass.

Peaches and Cream

**CLUB XIX AT THE LODGE
AT PEBBLE BEACH**
PEBBLE BEACH,
CALIFORNIA

1½ oz. Stolichnaya Persik Vodka
½ oz. Stolichnaya Vanil Vodka
1 peach slice for garnish

Stir or shake with ice. Strain and serve in a chilled martini glass. Garnish with the peach slice.

Pineapple Rum Martini

THE MARTINI CLUB
ATLANTA, GEORGIA

1 oz. Finlandia Pineapple Vodka
½ oz. Malibu Rum
1 oz. orange juice
1 orange slice for garnish

Stir with ice and strain into a chilled martini glass. Garnish with the orange slice.

Rainier Martini

**GARDEN COURT
AT THE FOUR SEASONS
OLYMPIC HOTEL**

SEATTLE, WASHINGTON

12 sour cherries

3 oz. Belvedere Vodka

1 Calvados-marinated Bing cherry for garnish

Combine sour cherries with the vodka and let stand for
24 hours. Stir well with ice and strain into an ice-cold martini
glass. Garnish with the Calvado-marinated Bing cherry.

Raspberry Martini

THE MARTINI CLUB

ATLANTA, GEORGIA

2¼ oz. Ketel One Vodka

¼ oz. Chambord raspberry liqueur

1 lemon twist for garnish

Stir with ice and strain into a chilled martini glass. Garnish
with the lemon twist.

Razamataz

**CLUB XIX AT THE LODGE
AT PEBBLE BEACH**

PEBBLE BEACH,
CALIFORNIA

1½ oz. Stolichnaya Razberi Vodka

½ oz. Stolichnaya Vanil Vodka

2 drops sweet and sour mix

3 fresh raspberries for garnish

Stir or shake vodkas and sweet and sour mix with ice. Strain
and serve. Garnish with the raspberries.

Romana Martini

TONGUE & GROOVE
ATLANTA, GEORGIA

1½ oz. premium vodka
½ oz. Romana Sambuca liqueur
3 coffee beans for garnish

Stir with ice and strain into a chilled martini glass. Garnish with the three coffee beans.

Sky Blue Martini

TONGUE & GROOVE
ATLANTA, GEORGIA

1½ oz. Skyy Vodka
½ oz. Blue Curaçao liqueur
1 orange slice for garnish

Stir with ice and strain into a chilled martini glass. Garnish with the orange slice.

Skyy Scraper

THE MARTINI CLUB
ATLANTA, GEORGIA

2½ oz. Skyy Vodka
3 olives for garnish

Stir with ice and strain into a chilled martini glass. Garnish with the olives skewered with a pick.

Sweet Cosmopolitan

TONGUE & GROOVE
ATLANTA, GEORGIA

1½ oz. premium vodka
¼ oz. Roses Lime Juice
¼ oz. Triple Sec
¼ oz. cranberry juice
¼ oz. sweet and sour mix
1 lemon twist for garnish

Stir with ice and strain into a chilled martini glass. Garnish with the lemon twist.

The 24-Karrot Martini

COMPASS ROSE
SAN FRANCISCO

2½ oz. Ketel One Vodka
1 pickled baby carrot for garnish

Stir with ice and strain into a chilled martini glass. Garnish with the pickled baby carrot.

Traditional Martini

**HARRY DENTON'S
STARLIGHT ROOM**
SAN FRANCISCO

2½ oz. Finlandia Vodka
1 Tony's Marinated Olive, for garnish (recipe follows)

Tony's Marinated Olives
Cocktail olives
Martini & Rossi Dry Vermouth
Cloves
Cinnamon sticks
Star Anise
Lemon zest

Shake with ice in a martini shaker and strain into a chilled martini glass. Garnish with the marinated olive.

Combine and marinate for 5 days.

Trai Cay Martini

LE COLONIAL

WEST HOLLYWOOD,
CALIFORNIA

1 oz. papaya juice

1 oz. Absolut Kurant Vodka

¾ oz. crème de banane liqueur

1 mint sprig for garnish

Pour over ice. Shake and serve in a chilled martini glass.
Garnish with the fresh sprig of mint.

MASON'S RESTAURANT

SAN FRANCISCO

1½ oz. vodka

½ oz. Godiva chocolate liqueur

½ oz. Frangelico liqueur*

1 mint sprig for garnish

Stir with ice and strain into a chilled martini glass. Garnish
with the mint sprig.

*Frangelico is a hazelnut-flavored liqueur enhanced with the essence
of flowers and berries.*

JOHNNY LOVE'S

SAN FRANCISCO

Touch of dry vermouth

2½ oz. Tanqueray Sterling Vodka

2 olives for garnish

Pour vermouth into a chilled glass and swirl it around. Dump
the vermouth into the sink. Chill the Tanqueray Sterling Vodka
until cold and strain into the glass. Garnish with the two olives
skewered on a pick.

White Chocolate Martini

COMPASS ROSE
SAN FRANCISCO

2½ oz. Ketel One Vodka

Splash of white crème de cacao

Stir with ice and strain into a chilled martini glass.

Wild Russians

THE COVEY
CARMEL, CALIFORNIA

2 oz. Stolichnaya Cristall Vodka

2 drops Framboise Eau de Vie*

1 raspberry for garnish

Fill shaker with ice. Add vodka and Framboise. Shake until well chilled. Strain into a martini glass. Garnish with the fresh raspberry.

Framboise Eau de Vie is colorless, potent and made from raspberries.

Julip Martini

MASON'S RESTAURANT
SAN FRANCISCO

1½ oz. gin or vodka
½ oz. Cointreau
1 mint sprig for garnish

Stir with ice and strain into a chilled martini glass. Garnish with the mint sprig.

Mint Martini

PRAVDA
NEW YORK CITY

3½ oz. gin or vodka
½ oz. Peppermint schnapps

Stir with ice and strain into a chilled martini glass.

Smokey Martini

PRAVDA
NEW YORK CITY

3¾ oz. gin or vodka
¼ oz. dry vermouth
Dash of Scotch

Stir with ice and strain into a chilled martini glass.

Tropical Martini

MASON'S RESTAURANT

SAN FRANCISCO

1½ oz. gin or vodka

¼ oz. Orgeat syrup (non-alcoholic)

¼ oz. Orange Curaçao

Splash of pineapple juice

1 lime slice for garnish

1 mint sprig for garnish

Stir with ice and strain into a chilled martini glass. Garnish with the lime slice and mint sprig.

Very Dirty Martini

PRAVDA

NEW YORK CITY

3¾ oz. gin or vodka

¼ oz. dry vermouth

Dash of olive juice

Stir with ice and strain into a chilled martini glass.

Glacier Blue

**GARDEN COURT
AT THE FOUR SEASONS
OLYMPIC HOTEL**

SEATTLE, WASHINGTON

1½ oz. Bombay Sapphire Gin
1½ oz. Stolichnaya Cristall Vodka
6 drops Blue Curaçao
1 orange twist for garnish

Spoon-twirl 40 revolutions with ice and strain into a chilled martini glass. Garnish with the orange twist.

James Bond

THE MARTINI CLUB
ATLANTA, GEORGIA

1¼ oz. Gordon's Gin
1¼ oz. Smirnoff Vodka
Splash of Lillet*
1 lemon twist for garnish

Stir with ice and strain into a chilled martini glass. Garnish with the lemon twist.

Lillet is a French apéritif made from a blend of wine, brandy, fruits and herbs.

Olympic Gold

**GARDEN COURT
AT THE FOUR SEASONS
OLYMPIC HOTEL**

SEATTLE, WASHINGTON

1 oz. Bombay Sapphire Gin
1½ oz. Absolut Citron Vodka
⅓ oz. Canton
1/6 oz. Martell Cordon Bleu
1 lemon twist for garnish

Spoon-twirl 40 revolutions with ice and strain into a chilled martini glass. Garnish with the lemon twist.

The 007—Shaken, not Stirred

THE VIPER ROOM

WEST HOLLYWOOD, CALIFORNIA

3 oz. gin
1 oz. vodka
½ oz. Lillet*

Shake with ice and strain into a chilled martini glass.
Note: This is James Bond's original martini. It appeared in Casino Royal. James calls this "The Vesper."

Lillet is a French apéritif made from a blend of wine, brandy, fruits and herbs.

Veloz Martini

SAN YSIDRO RANCH

SANTA BARBARA, CALIFORNIA

1 oz. Ketel One Vodka
1 oz. Bombay Sapphire Gin
1 lemon twist for garnish

Pour ingredients into shaker with ice. Shake for 15 seconds and strain into a well-chilled martini glass. Garnish with the lemon twist.

Other Liqueurs

Jamaican Martini

THE MARTINI CLUB
ATLANTA, GEORGIA

1 oz. Mount Gay Rum
1 oz. orange juice
½ oz. pineapple juice
1 orange slice for garnish

Stir with ice and strain into a chilled martini glass. Garnish with the orange slice.

Whisky Manhattan

THE MARTINI CLUB
ATLANTA, GEORGIA

2¼ oz. Maker's Mark Whisky
¼ oz. sweet vermouth
1 cherry for garnish

Stir with ice and strain into a chilled martini glass. Garnish with the cherry.

Manhattan Martini

THE VIPER ROOM
WEST HOLLYWOOD,
CALIFORNIA

2½ oz. Maker's Mark Bourbon
Splash of sweet vermouth

Stir with ice and strain into a chilled martini glass.

Appetizer
Recipes

Barbecued Duck Taco with Tomatillo Salsa

SERVES 8
PREPARATION TIME:
30 MINUTES
(NOTE CURING TIME)
PREHEAT OVEN TO 400°

4 **duck legs, skinned,**
   8 oz. each

1½ **cups kosher salt**

1 **Tbsp. fresh thyme,**
  chopped

16 **black peppercorns**

2 **bay leaves,**
  chopped

4 **cups bacon fat**

4 **cups goose fat,**
  duck fat or pork fat

1 **garlic clove**

1 **onion, sliced**

1 **carrot, chopped**

1 **celery stalk,**
  roughly chopped

1 **qt. water**

1 **cup apple cider**
  vinegar

4 **ancho chiles**

4 **guajillo chiles***

¼ **cup honey**

Tomatillo salsa
(recipe follows)

8 **flour tortillas**

1 **cup Jack cheese,**
  grated

1 **cup spinach,**
  julienned

1 **cup pico de gallo**
  (optional)

Place skinned duck legs in a mixing bowl and add the salt, chopped thyme, cracked black peppercorns and bay leaves. Toss together and lay on an icing rack. Place icing rack on sheet pan and place in refrigerator for 24 hours to cure.

Place bacon fat and goose fat, garlic and vegetables in a 6-qt. kettle over low heat. Place duck legs in fat. The fat should cover the legs. Bring fat to 180° and cook for 2 to 2½ hours. When duck meat is falling from the bone, remove from the fat. Raise heat to high and cook the fat at 300° to 325° for 4 to 6 minutes or until all liquid has evaporated. Strain through a fine sieve. Refrigerate fat for next time. The fat may be kept for two or more months.

For the barbecue sauce, bring the water to a boil with salt and cider vinegar.

Stem, split and seed dried chiles. Lay the chiles on a sheet pan or cookie sheet and toast in a 400° oven for 45 seconds to 1 minute. Place the chiles in a 2 qt. mixing bowl and pour the boiling water over them. Let stand for 5 minutes. Remove the chiles from the hot water and place in a blender with honey and 1½ cups of the water-vinegar mixture. Blend until smooth, adding more water if necessary.

Heat the duck meat in the barbecue sauce.

Ladle ¼ cup tomatillo salsa (recipe follows) onto each plate. Lay the heated tortilla flat on a plate or work surface and top with 2 to 4 Tbsps. duck meat. Top with Jack cheese and julienned spinach. Roll tortilla up tightly and place on top of the tomatillo sauce. Garnish with pico de gallo.

Guajillo chiles are pointed, long and narrow, with shiny-smooth, burnished red skin. They are quite hot.

Tomatillo Salsa

PUT THE TOMATILLOS in a 4 qt. pan and top with 1 qt. of water. Add the salt, jalapeño pepper, onion and garlic. Slowly cook for 15 minutes. Remove from heat.

Place the tomatillos, onion and jalapeño in a blender. Add ½ cup of the liquid and blend until smooth. You may need to add more liquid. Add chopped cilantro just before serving.

PREPARATION TIME:
30 MINUTES

16 medium-sized tomatillos, removed from husk

1 qt. water

Kosher salt to taste

½ jalapeño pepper

½ yellow onion, peeled and roughly chopped

2 garlic cloves

1 Tbsp. cilantro, chopped

Basil Pesto Dip with Crackers

YIELD: 1½ CUPS
PREPARATION TIME:
15 MINUTES

3 garlic cloves, minced

½ cup fresh basil leaves, firmly packed

2 Tbsps. almonds, blanched

2 Tbsps. olive oil

½ cup Parmesan cheese, grated

16 oz. ricotta cheese, at room temperature

¼ cup almonds, slivered

PLACE THE GARLIC, basil and blanched almonds in the bowl of a food processor or in a blender. With the motor running, slowly drizzle in the oil through the feed tube; process until the basil is pureed. Transfer the pesto to a bowl and stir in the Parmesan cheese. Add salt and pepper, if desired, to taste. Refrigerate, covered, until ready to use. Keeps in the refrigerator for 2 to 3 days.

With a mixer or food processor, beat ricotta and pesto until well blended. Cover and chill until ready to use.

To serve, plate the dip and sprinkle with slivered almonds. Serve with crackers on the side.

Bay Scallops and Mandarin Orange Skewers

SERVES 4
PREPARATION TIME:
20 MINUTES
(NOTE MARINATING TIME)

In a medium-sized bowl, combine the dry Riesling, orange juice, orange rind, soy sauce, garlic, ginger, ½ tsp. honey and ½ tsp. of the mustard. Add the scallops and toss to coat. Refrigerate, covered, for 2 hours or overnight.

Preheat the barbecue. Drain the scallops, reserving some of the liquid for basting. In a small bowl, toss the scallops with the oil. Place the scallops in a small boat made out of heavy-duty

aluminum foil. Add a small amount of the reserved liquid and place foil packet on grill. Cook for 6 to 8 minutes or until scallops are firm. Drain.

Meanwhile, in a small bowl, whisk the mayonnaise with the remaining ½ tsp. each of honey and mustard, lime juice and a touch of horseradish; transfer to a serving dish.

Arrange 2 bay scallops alternately with 2 mandarin orange segments on wooden skewers until all the scallops and orange segments are used. Arrange the skewers around a platter and serve with the seasoned mayonnaise in the center for dipping.

- ¼ cup dry Riesling
- ¼ cup orange juice
- 2 tsps. grated orange rind
- 2 tsps. soy sauce
- 1 garlic clove, minced
- ½ tsp. fresh ginger, minced
- 1 tsp. honey, divided
- 1 tsp. Dijon mustard, divided
- 1 lb. bay scallops
- 2 tsps. sesame oil or peanut oil
- ¼ cup mayonnaise
  Juice from ¼ lime
  Horseradish, to taste
- 1 can (11 oz.) mandarin oranges, drained

Blue Cheese Meatballs

YIELD:
75 BITE-SIZED
MEATBALLS
PREPARATION TIME:
30 MINUTES
PREHEAT OVEN TO 350°

1 lb. lean ground beef

6 oz. blue cheese, crumbled

1 tsp. salt, optional

1 small garlic clove, minced

½ cup bread crumbs

¼ tsp. oregano

¼ tsp. rosemary

2 Tbsps. parsley, chopped

¾ cup Pinot Gris wine

¼ cup oil

In a large mixing bowl, combine the beef, blue cheese, salt, garlic, bread crumbs, oregano, rosemary, parsley and ½ cup of the wine. Mix well.

Shape mixture into small, bite-sized balls (about 1 tsp. each).

Brown the meatballs well on all sides in oil over medium heat. Remove from heat and drain on paper towels. Refrigerate until ready to use.

Prior to serving, place the meatballs in a shallow casserole or chafing dish. Add the remaining ¼ cup wine and bake in a 350° oven for 15 minutes or until heated through.

These meatballs can be made larger and served as a main dish with spaghetti.

Bruschetta with Gorgonzola and Walnuts

SAUTÉ THE GARLIC in olive oil. Remove from pan.
Mix the Gorgonzola and mascarpone cheese together until creamy. Add the walnuts.

Toast the bread on a grill. Rub the garlic on the toast, then drizzle with olive oil and spread the cheese.

Sprinkle parsley on top and serve.

**SERVES 4
PREPARATION TIME:
10 MINUTES**

1 **garlic clove, chopped**

2 **tsps. olive oil**

4 **oz. Gorgonzola cheese**

4 **oz. mascarpone cheese**

⅛ **cup walnuts, finely chopped**

4 **slices of bread**

Parsley, chopped, for garnish

Ceviche of Striped Bass and Scallops

SERVES 4
PREPARATION TIME:
15 MINUTES
(NOTE MARINATING TIME)

- 4 Tbsps. lime juice
- 7 oz. sea bass, skinless, boneless and cut on a slight bias
- ½ lb. scallops
- ½ tsp. salt
- 1 cup tomato, seeded and diced
- ¼ cup red onion, minced
- ½ Tbsp. jalapeño, seeded and minced
- 1 Tbsp. oregano, chopped
- 1 Tbsp. cilantro, chopped

PLACE LIME JUICE in a bowl. Cut the bass into pieces the size of scallops.

Slice scallops crosswise to ⅛ inch thick. Add the bass and the scallops to the bowl with the lime juice. Add salt and toss well. Refrigerate for 1 hour.

In a separate bowl, combine the diced tomato, onion, jalapeño, oregano and cilantro. When the fish and scallops have marinated for 1 hour, toss gently with the tomato mixture. Refrigerate an additional hour.

Arrange bass and scallops on a well-chilled platter. Drizzle the marinade over the fish before serving.

Chicken Drumsticks with Merlot and Blackberries

SERVES 4
PREPARATION TIME:
45 MINUTES
PREHEAT OVEN TO 375°

PLACE THE DRUMSTICKS in a buttered baking dish. Pour ¼ cup of wine over the chicken, sprinkle with paprika, thyme, salt and pepper.

Bake in a 375° oven for 15 minutes.

Remove the chicken from the oven and baste with the remaining ¼ cup Merlot. Return the chicken to the oven for an additional 10 minutes.

Combine the brown sugar, blackberry jam, cumin, garlic, olive oil and vinegar. Cover the drumsticks on all sides with half of the blackberry mixture, using a pastry brush. Return to the oven for another 10 minutes.

Spoon remaining blackberry mixture over the drumsticks before serving.

3 to 4 lbs. chicken drumsticks

½ cup Merlot

1 tsp. paprika

1½ tsps. thyme leaves
  Salt and pepper to taste

2 Tbsps. brown sugar

½ cup seedless blackberry jam

½ tsp. ground cumin

2 garlic cloves, minced

1 tsp. olive oil

2 Tbsps. white wine vinegar

Chicken Kabobs

SERVES 2
PREPARATION TIME:
30 MINUTES
(NOTE MARINATING TIME)

½ **lemon, juiced**

2 **Tbsps. sesame oil**

1 **garlic clove, peeled and finely chopped**

Pinch of fresh ginger, finely grated

2 **chicken breasts, boneless and skinless**

1 **shallot, peeled and finely chopped**

1 **red sweet pepper, seeds removed, diced into ½-inch cubes**

¼ **cup white wine**

½ **cup chicken stock**

1 **medium-sized tomato, peeled, seeded and coarsely chopped**

Salt and pepper to taste

2 **Tbsps. plain yogurt**

2 **Tbsps. pine nuts, toasted and coarsely chopped**

1 **tsp. fresh basil, finely chopped**

1 **onion, peeled**

2 **skewers**

2 **Tbsps. olive oil**

In a large bowl, combine the lemon juice, 2 Tbsps. sesame oil, garlic and ginger for the marinade.

Cut the chicken into 1¼-inch cubes and add to the marinade. Mix well to coat. Cover and refrigerate for at least 1 hour.

Heat a nonstick pan over medium heat. Add the chicken cubes and cook for approximately 2 minutes or until golden brown. Remove from the pan and place on paper towels. Set aside.

Heat 2 Tbsps. sesame oil in a saucepan. Add the shallot and 1 red pepper that is diced and seeded and sweat for 2 minutes. Add the white wine and chicken stock and bring to a boil. Reduce the heat, cover and simmer until the pepper is completely cooked.

Purée the mixture and pass through a fine sieve into a clean saucepan. Add the chopped tomato and bring back to a boil. Season with salt and freshly ground pepper and remove from the heat. Add the yogurt, pine nuts and basil. Set aside.

Cut 1 red pepper into 1¼-inch square shapes. Cut the onion into similar pieces. Drop into boiling salted water and blanch for 2 minutes, taking care that they remain crisp. Remove and refresh in a bowl of iced water. Drain and dry on paper towels.

Thread a piece of chicken onto a skewer, followed by a piece of onion and a piece of pepper. Continue until all the chicken and vegetables are used up. Make sure they are not pressed too tightly against each other.

Season the kabobs and brush with olive oil. Then place on a baking tray and grill for 5 to 8 minutes or until medium-well done.

Country Pâté

SEPARATE THE BACON SLICES and blanch them in boiling water for 1 minute to remove excess salt. Rinse in warm water and drain.

Line the bottom and sides of a loaf pan with the bacon slices, letting the bacon hang over the edges of the pan. Place 2 bay leaves on top of the bacon. Set aside.

Tear the bread in pieces and place in a small bowl. Add the cream and port or cognac to the bread and let soak until the bread has absorbed the liquids.

Coarsely grind the raw chicken livers and then mix the liver with the pork sausage in a large bowl. Add the saturated bread, the herbs, spices and garlic and blend until combined.

Sauté 2 Tbsps. of the pâté mixture in a skillet and taste; adjust seasonings.

Spoon the pâté into the prepared loaf pan and place the remaining 2 bay leaves on top. Fold the overhanging bacon strips onto the top of the pâté and cover with any remaining bacon slices.

Cover the pâté with a piece of aluminum foil and place in a bain-marie or water bath. To fabricate a bain-marie, simply fill a pan larger in all dimensions than the loaf pan with boiling water to halfway up the sides of the pâté. Place the loaf pan in the center of the water bath and bake for 1¾ hours or until the internal temperature reaches 160°.

Remove the pâté from the oven and let cool for 15 minutes on a wire rack. Compress the pâté by weighting it with a brick or cans for at least 1 hour. When cool, unmold the pâté and wrap tightly in aluminum foil. Refrigerate 2 days before serving to allow flavors to develop, or freeze for up to 3 months.

To serve, discard the bay leaves and any excess bacon. Slice the pâté with a serrated knife and serve with condiments such as Dijon mustard, sliced Bermuda onion, cornichons (French sour pickles), capers or sliced tomatoes. Serve it on pumpernickel bread, crackers or wafers.

YIELD: 1 LOAF
PREPARATION TIME:
1½ HOURS
COOKING TIME:
1¾ HOURS
(NOTE REFRIGERATION TIME)
PREHEAT OVEN TO 325°

1 lb. bacon, sliced

4 bay leaves

4 slices white bread, crust removed

½ cup heavy cream

½ cup port or cognac

1 lb. chicken livers, rinsed and drained

1½ lb. pork sausage

1 tsp. thyme

¼ tsp. allspice

¼ tsp. white pepper

¼ tsp. nutmeg

1 garlic clove, minced

Crab Meat Spring Roll and Tamari Sauce

SERVES 8
PREPARATION TIME:
30 MINUTES

4 oz. Maine crab meat

2 tsps. shallots, minced

2 Tbsps. crème fraîche

1 Tbsp. dill, chopped

1 Tbsp. tarragon, chopped

1 Tbsp. chives, chopped

Salt and pepper to taste

16 spring roll wrappers

2 eggs, beaten

¼ cup tamari soy

1 Granny Smith apple, roughly chopped

1 tsp. ginger

½ garlic clove

2 Tbsps. onion, roughly chopped

⅓ cup rice wine vinegar

¼ cup peanut oil

Olive oil for sautéing

In a large mixing bowl, gently combine the crab meat with the shallots, crème fraîche and spices. Season to taste.

Lay out spring roll wrappers. Brush edges with egg. Place crab meat in center and roll tightly.

For the dipping sauce, place tamari soy and remaining ingredients in a blender and blend until smooth. Season to taste.

Heat olive oil in a pan and add the spring rolls, a few at a time. Cook until golden on all sides. Slice and serve with dipping sauce.

Crab Toast

MELT THE SOFTENED CREAM CHEESE with the heavy cream over low heat. Stir until smooth.

In a separate pan, sauté the garlic and shallot approximately 1 minute. Add to the cream cheese mixture and stir well. Heat through and remove from heat.

Add the herbs and seasonings and blend well.

Gently fold in the crab meat, preserving the integrity of the lumps. Taste and adjust the seasonings as necessary.

Serve on toast wedges.

SERVES 4
PREPARATION TIME:
15 MINUTES

8 oz. well-softened cream cheese

½ cup heavy cream

2 garlic cloves, minced

1 shallot, minced

4 leaves basil, minced

2 Tbsps. chives, minced

Salt and pepper to taste

Cayenne pepper to taste

Old Bay seasoning (for authentic Maryland Style flavor)

1 lb. jumbo lump crab meat, picked

8 slices of toast

Crispy Pan-Fried Oysters

SERVES 6
PREPARATION TIME:
25 MINUTES

Oysters

3 **dozen oysters,
   shucked**

3 **parts flour**

1 **part horseradish**

**Vegetable oil for
frying**

Sauce

**Peel of two
cucumbers**

1 **egg yolk**

¼ **cup rice wine
vinegar**

½ **cup olive oil**

½ **cup vegetable oil**

**Salt and pepper to
taste**

Fresh dill to taste

**Salmon caviar for
garnish (optional)**

Coat shucked oysters in a mixture of 3 parts flour to one part horseradish. Pan fry in vegetable oil until crispy and brown.

Sauce

Cut the cucumbers in half. Scoop out seeds to form a shell.

In a bowl, mix egg yolk, rice wine vinegar, olive oil, vegetable oil, salt, pepper and dill in a blender until smooth. Place sauce in the bottom of each cucumber shell. Place oyster in shell and top with a dollop of salmon caviar.

Eggplant Caviar

SERVES 4
PREPARATION TIME:
25 MINUTES

PRICK THE EGGPLANT several times with a fork. In a broiler or on a flat griddle or grill, roast the eggplant until the skin begins to blacken, the juices turn syrupy and the pulp feels completely soft.

Cool until touchable. Peel the eggplant and roughly chop the pulp.

Place the eggplant in a bowl and add the onion, garlic and tomato. Stir until smooth. Add the olive oil, salt, pepper and lemon juice to taste. Garnish with the herbs.

- 1 **large eggplant**
- ½ **small red onion, chopped**
- ¼ **tsp. garlic, minced**
- ½ **tomato, peeled and seeded**
- 2 **Tbsps. olive oil**
- **Salt and pepper to taste**
- **Juice of ½ lemon**
- 2 **Tbsps. parsley, chopped**
- **Fresh basil, chopped (optional)**

Eggplant Chicken (Nasu Hasami Yaki)

SERVES 4

PREPARATION TIME:
20 MINUTES

PREHEAT OVEN TO 400°

4 **Japanese eggplants, each 5-inches long, or 1 medium Italian eggplant**

⅓ **cup soy sauce**

5 **tsps. sugar**

2 **Tbsps. mirin,* sake or sherry**

2 **tsps. cornstarch**

1 **tsp. ginger, fresh or powdered**

4 **chicken breast fillets, 1-inch wide, boned and skinned**

Shredded lettuce for garnish

Tomato for garnish

REMOVE STEMS of the Japanese eggplants. Make a shallow cut around the eggplant 1½-inches from the stem end. Leave skin on stem end, peel balance of the skin. Split the eggplant on the peeled end only. If using Italian eggplant, follow the same procedure but quarter lengthwise.

To make the yakitori sauce, heat soy sauce and sugar. Add the mirin, cornstarch and ginger and bring to a boil.

Fit the two halves of the butterflied eggplants around the chicken fillets. Place on an oiled cookie sheet and bake for 12 minutes at 400° or until tender.

Baste with the yakitori sauce. Garnish with the lettuce and tomato.

* Mirin is a low-alcohol, sweet golden wine made from glutinous rice.

Ethiopian Chicken Legs

SERVES 12
PREPARATION TIME:
1 HOUR
(NOTE REFRIGERATION
TIME)
PREHEAT OVEN TO 375°

To PREPARE the *berbere* place all of the dried spices in a small skillet and cook over low heat, stirring constantly, for 4 to 5 minutes. The spices should become fragrant and hot to the touch. Add the red wine and stir to make a paste. Remove the skillet from the stove and add the orange juice and oil.

Dry the chicken legs with paper towels and then liberally coat the meat with the spice paste. Place the chicken in a plastic bag or in a baking pan, covered with plastic wrap, and chill for at least 24 hours.

When you are ready to cook the chicken, preheat oven to 375°. Arrange the drumsticks on a baking tray so the pieces do not touch or crowd one another.

Bake for 30 to 40 minutes or until cooked through, turning the chicken once during the cooking process. The cooking time will vary depending on the size of the drumsticks.

½ tsp. ground ginger

½ tsp. ground cardamom

1 tsp. ground coriander

½ Tbsp. ground turmeric

½ Tbsp. dry mustard powder

½ tsp. ground nutmeg

½ tsp. ground allspice

½ tsp. ground cinnamon

¼ cup Hungarian hot paprika

1 Tbsp. cayenne pepper

1½ tsps. salt

⅓ cup red wine

2 Tbsps. orange juice

2 Tbsps. peanut oil

24 small chicken legs

Goat Cheese Spring Rolls

SERVES 4
PREPARATION TIME: 30
MINUTES

1½ cups goat cheese
½ tsp. garlic, chopped
½ tsp. fresh tarragon, chopped
1 Tbsp. parsley, chopped
1 green onion, thinly sliced
1½ tsps. kalamata olives, chopped
1 Tbsp. sun-dried tomatoes, chopped
1½ tsps. olive oil
½ tsp. black peppercorns, crushed
1 egg, beaten
12 spring-roll wrappers
Oil for deep frying

Mix all the ingredients together except the egg, wrappers and oil.

Place a spoonful of the mixture on one corner of each spring-roll wrapper. Fold in the sides and roll.

Brush the edges of each wrapper with the beaten egg to seal.

Deep fry rolls until golden brown. Place on paper to absorb excess oil.

COOKING SECRET

Serve as an appetizer or accompaniment with a spinach salad or pasta.

Honeyed Teriyaki Chicken Nuggets

COMBINE THE SALT, pepper and flour in a medium-sized plastic bag and shake to blend.

Dip the chicken into beaten egg, then drop into the plastic bag and shake well to coat with seasoned flour.

Heat the oil until hot and add the chicken to fill pan. Cook, turning as needed, until chicken is golden brown, about 5 to 8 minutes, depending on size of chunks.

While the chicken is cooking, heat the soy, honey, red wine, garlic and ginger in a small saucepan, until the ingredients are warm and blended together.

When the chicken is crisp and golden brown, remove from the skillet and drain on paper towels. Dip in honey mixture to coat well, then put on a broiler pan or a rack set into a baking pan. Bake at 250° for 20 minutes, brushing with glaze after 10 minutes.

SERVES 4
PREPARATION TIME:
30 MINUTES

½ tsp. salt

⅛ tsp. pepper

½ cup flour

2 lbs. chicken breasts cut into 2-inch chunks

2 eggs, beaten
   Oil for frying

⅓ cup soy sauce

⅓ cup honey

1 Tbsp. dry red wine

1 garlic clove

1 tsp. fresh ginger, grated

Italian White Bean Cakes

**SERVES 6
PREPARATION TIME:
1¾ HOURS
(NOTE REFRIGERATION
TIME)**

1 cup dried white beans, soaked and drained

1 Tbsp. olive oil

½ medium onion, diced

1 garlic clove, minced

2 Tbsps. parsley, minced

¾ Tbsp. fresh sage, minced

¾ Tbsp. salt

¼ Tbsp. fresh ground black pepper

1 cup flour

3 Tbsps. vegetable oil

½ lb. mustard greens, julienned

Cucumbers, olives and peppers in lemon vinaigrette (recipe follows)

Cook the beans in 4 cups water until tender, about 1 hour. Remove 1 cup of beans from pot, chop coarsely and set aside.

Continue cooking the remaining beans until very soft. Drain and purée until smooth. Set aside.

Heat olive oil in a sauté pan over medium heat. Sauté onion and garlic until translucent. Add parsley, sage, salt and pepper. Mix with the puréed and chopped beans. Taste for seasoning. Chill the mixture for 1 hour.

Put flour in a shallow dish. Flour your hands, scoop out approximately ⅓ cup of the bean mixture, shape into a 3-inch cake about 1 inch thick.

Set the bean cake in the shallow dish and dust with flour.

Cook over low heat in the sauté pan in a the vegetable oil for 4 minutes, then turn over and cook about 5 minutes more, or until golden brown.

Serve immediately on a bed of julienned mustard greens, with cucumbers, olives and peppers in lemon vinaigrette.

Cucumber, olives and peppers in lemon vinaigrette

Juice from 4 lemons

2 Tbsps. olive oil

2 cucumbers, peeled, seeded and thinly sliced

1 red pepper, seeded and sliced

½ cup kalamata olives, pitted and sliced

Salt and pepper to taste

Mix lemon juice and olive oil. Add cucumbers, red pepper and olives. Season to taste. Marinate for about 1 hour.

Garnish bean cakes with cucumber mixture. Drizzle the vinaigrette over the bean cakes.

Salmon Buckwheat Blini and Asian Salad

SERVES 4
PREPARATION TIME:
45 MINUTES
(NOTE STANDING TIME)

IN A LARGE SAUCEPAN, warm the milk over low heat. Remove from heat and add the yeast. Let stand for at least ½ hour. Add the flours and let stand for 2 hours. Add the egg yolks to the flour mixture. Whip the egg whites to soft peaks and fold into the flour mixture. Add salt to taste. Add melted butter and mix well. Set aside.

In a small saucepan, bring the vinegar to a boil. Add the red onion to the vinegar. Remove the saucepan from the heat and let stand 15 minutes or until cool. Set aside.

Make the seasoning salt in a small sauté pan by combining the kosher salt, star anise, black pepper and cloves and heating until they are warm. Pour these dry ingredients into a coffee grinder and process until powdered. Set aside.

For the smoking mixture, combine the jasmine tea, brown sugar and rice and set aside.

For the balsamic vinegar syrup, combine the balsamic vinegar and sugar together in a small sauté pan, bring to a simmer and reduce by ⅓. Cool.

In a Teflon pan, put a small amount of cooking spray or butter. Add enough batter to make two ½-inch to 3-inch pancakes. Cook the blini the way you would a pancake. Remove to a separate plate. Pour the excess vinegar off the onions and add the julienned cucumber. Set the salad aside.

Season the salmon with some of the seasoning salt and let stand for at least 1 hour. Line the bottom of the sauté pan with aluminum foil and pour the smoking mixture in the pan. Place the salmon in a Chinese steaming basket and place the basket in the sauté pan over the smoking mixture. Wrap the foil up over the top of the steaming basket and turn the heat on medium high. Smoke the fish for approximately 10 to 15 minutes or until done.

Place the blini in the center of the plate with the salad mixture on top of the blini. Place one piece of the salmon on top of the salad. Lightly drizzle the syrup over the top of the salmon.

1¾ cups milk

1 tsp. dry yeast

1½ cups flour

½ cup buckwheat flour

3 eggs, separated

1 tsp. salt

1 Tbsp. butter, melted

1½ cups seasoned rice vinegar

2 red onions, julienned

½ cup kosher salt

1 Tbsp. star anise

½ tsp. black pepper

4 cloves

1 cup jasmine tea

½ cup brown sugar

½ cup rice

1 cup balsamic vinegar

¾ cup sugar

1 English cucumber, julienned

½ lb. salmon, cut into triangles, 2 oz. per person

Lobster and Corn Fritters

SERVES 4
PREPARATION TIME:
20 MINUTES

½ **cup flour**

¼ **tsp. salt**

2 **tsps. baking powder**

½ **cup milk**

1 **egg, lightly beaten**

Meat of 1 whole lobster, cooked

1 **cup corn kernels or 1 cup yam, raw and shredded**

Pepper to taste

Oil for frying

Fresh cilantro leaves for garnish

In a mixing bowl combine the flour, salt and baking powder.

In another bowl, stir together the milk and egg. Gradually add the milk mixture to the flour, stirring just until mixture is smooth. Stir in the lobster and corn or yam. Pepper to taste.

In a large skillet add enough oil to cover the bottom of the pan. Ladle the batter onto the hot oil to form 4 large fritters, about 3 inches wide. Fry for 3 minutes on the first side, then about 2 minutes on the other side.

Garnish with cilantro and serve.

Lobster in Mango Cups

SERVES 2
PREPARATION TIME:
2 HOURS

Cut mangoes in half the long way and remove seeds. Remove the mango meat in strips and set the mango cups aside.

Melt 2 Tbsps. butter in a heavy frying pan over medium heat and brown the garlic. Add lobster meat and sauté quickly for 30 seconds. Pour brandy over the lobster and flambé. Remove from heat and set aside.

Melt ½ cup butter in saucepan and slowly add the flour, stirring thoroughly until smooth. Slowly add the water and cook over low heat for 20 minutes, until reduced to 1 cup.

Add curry powder, mango purée, pineapple juice, catsup, wine and cream. Stir and cook 2 minutes over low heat.

Add Tabasco, salt, pepper and lobster, stirring for 1 minute.

Pour into mango cups and garnish with mango strips on top.

2 ripe, fresh mangoes

½ cup + 2 Tbsps. butter

2 garlic cloves, minced

½ lb. lobster meat, diced

¼ cup brandy

½ cup all-purpose flour

2 cups water

1 tsp. curry powder

2 tsps. mango purée

½ cup pineapple juice

4 tsps. catsup

¼ cup white wine

¼ cup heavy cream

2 drops Tabasco sauce

½ tsp. salt

White pepper to taste

Lobster Tamale

SERVES 10
PREPARATION TIME:
1 HOUR
PREHEAT OVEN TO 350°

1 **lb. masa**

1 **lemon, zested and chopped**

2 **ears fresh sweet corn, removed from cob**

2 **Tbsps. parsley, chopped**

   Kosher salt to taste

   Pepper to taste

3 **gals. water**

1 **onion, chopped**

1 **celery stalk, chopped**

5 **white peppercorns**

1 **carrot, chopped**

1 **bay leaf**

2 **sprigs fresh thyme**

5 **Maine lobsters, 1 lb. each**

   Large container with ice water

1 **package dry corn husks**

   Lobster Tamale Sauce (recipe follows on next page)

In a large mixing bowl combine the masa, lemon, corn, parsley, salt and pepper. Set aside.

Boil the water with the onion, celery, peppercorns, carrot, bay leaf and thyme. Season with salt and let simmer for 10 minutes.

Return to high heat and add the lobsters, cooking for 5 minutes. Remove lobsters and plunge into ice water. Let stand for 15 minutes.

Remove lobster meat and claw meat from shells, reserving lobster heads for the sauce. Cut each tail in half lengthwise and then each half into 6 pieces. Reserve claws and heads and refrigerate until needed.

Reconstitute the corn husks in warm water until pliable. Spread 3 to 4 Tbsps. of the masa mixture on each corn husk. Place half a lobster tail on the masa and roll up into tamale. Steam for 15 to 20 minutes.

To serve, heat the remaining lobster in a 350° oven for 3 minutes. Meanwhile, remove tamales from husks and place on warm plates. Ladle the sauce over the tamales and garnish with remaining lobster.

Lobster Tamale Sauce

HEAT OIL IN A WIDE-BOTTOMED PAN until very hot. Add the crushed lobster heads, a little at a time, making sure not to cool down the pan too much. Stir and cook for 5 minutes.

Add the onion, celery and carrot. Continue stirring and cook for 2 minutes.

Add the chicken stock, tomato paste and chipotle chiles. Cook over low heat for 15 minutes. Blend, strain and reserve.

Combine the wine, bay leaf, shallots, peppercorns and thyme in a nonreactive saucepan. Reduce over high heat until 1 Tbsp. remains. Add the heavy cream and reduce over high heat until the cream coats the back of a spoon. Strain and blend with the reserved sauce. Season with salt and keep warm.

**PREPARATION TIME:
20 MINUTES**

¼ cup vegetable oil

5 lobster heads, crushed

1 onion, peeled and sliced

1 celery stalk, chopped

1 carrot, peeled and chopped

6 cups chicken stock

1 Tbsp. tomato paste

2 chipotle chiles, seeded

2 cups white wine

1 bay leaf

6 shallots, sliced

6 white peppercorns

1 sprig fresh thyme

2 qts. heavy cream

Salt to taste

Maine Crab Cakes

SERVES 8
PREPARATION TIME:
30 MINUTES

1½ lbs. crab

1 Tbsp. red pepper, finely diced

1 Tbsp. green pepper, finely diced

1 Tbsp. yellow pepper, finely diced

1 Tbsp. parsley, finely diced

3 Tbsps. onion, diced and sautéed

½ cup seasoned bread crumbs

½ cup Parmesan cheese

1 whole egg

6 drops Tabasco sauce

2 tsps. lemon juice

1 Tbsp. mayonnaise

Butter for sautéing

Lemon wedges

MIX CRAB MEAT, peppers, parsley, onion, bread crumbs, Parmesan, egg, Tabasco, lemon juice and mayonniase together in a bowl. Form the crab mixture into 2 oz. patties.

Heat butter in a medium-sized skillet and cook the crab cakes over medium heat until golden on both sides, about 3 minutes per side.

Serve hot with lemon wedges.

Mushroom Mini Rolls

SERVES 4
PREPARATION TIME:
35 MINUTES
PREHEAT OVEN TO 400°

Sauté the mushrooms in butter until soft. Remove from heat and add soup, onions and almonds.

Cut phyllo sheets into quarters. Place a generous tablespoon of mushroom filling on each sheet and roll up, egg-roll style.

Place on baking sheet sprayed with a non-stick spray. Brush the tops with melted butter. Bake at 400° for 15 to 20 minutes, until golden brown.

Serve hot or at room temperature.

COOKING SECRET

Can be prepared, rolled ahead and frozen—then baked before serving.

1 lb. mushrooms, sliced

2 Tbsps. butter

1 can undiluted mushroom soup

2 green onions, sliced

½ cup almonds, sliced

1 package phyllo dough

¼ cup butter, melted

Nordic Toast

SERVES 4
PREPARATION TIME:
35 MINUTES

1 Tbsp. sweet
   mustard

½ tsp. mustard
   powder

1 Tbsp. white sugar

1 tsp. white vinegar

½ cup peanut oil

   Pinch of salt

4 slices Alaska cold-
   smoked salmon

4 slices white bread

6 Tbsps. clarified
   butter

2 Tbsps. sour cream

1 tsp. horseradish,
   grated

2 Tbsps. lime juice

3 Tbsps. olive oil

4 leaves butter
   lettuce

2 eggs, hard boiled,
   quartered

1 lemon, cut into
   wedges

1 Tbsp. chives,
   chopped

4 sprigs dill

COMBINE IN A BLENDER the sweet mustard, mustard powder, sugar, vinegar, oil and salt. Pulse for 20 seconds. Spread the smoked salmon. Set aside.

Deep fry the bread in the clarified butter in a sauté pan. Set aside on paper towels to blot up excess oil.

Combine the sour cream and horseradish in a bowl. Mix in the lime juice and olive oil. Set aside.

Place the lettuce leaves on individual serving plates and top with the toast. Add the salmon coated with mustard mixture. Garnish with the egg quarters and lemon wedges. Top with the horseradish cream. Garnish with chopped chives and sprigs of dill.

Oyster Six Shot

SERVES 4
PREPARATION TIME:
45 MINUTES

For the Peppercorn Mignonette: Combine all the ingredients except the oil in a blender. With the blender still running, slowly add the oil to emulsify. Set aside.

For the Cajun-Mary Sauce: In a mixing bowl combine all the ingredients. Season to taste with salt, pepper and Creole seasoning.

To assemble, place 1 oyster in each of the 24 shot glasses. Top 12 of the oysters with 1 Tbsp. of the Peppercorn Mignonette. Top the other 12 with 1 Tbsp. of the Cajun-Mary Sauce.

Place 6 shot glasses on each of 4 large plates: 3 with Peppercorn Mignonette and 3 with Cajun-Mary Sauce. Garnish with a lemon crown in the center of the plate and a sprinkling of parsley.

Peppercorn Mignonette
YIELD: 1½ CUPS

- 2 shallots, peeled, minced
- ½ cup red wine vinegar
- 5 Tbsps. Creole mustard
- 1 Tbsp. cracked black pepper
- 1 tsp. salt
- 1½ cups salad oil

Cajun-Mary Sauce
YIELD: 1½ CUPS

- 1 cup tomato juice
- ½ cup tomato paste
- 1 tsp. Tabasco sauce
- 3 Tbsps. Worcestershire sauce
- ¼ cup lemon juice
- ½ tsp. ground celery seeds
- Salt and black pepper to taste
- Creole seasoning to taste
- 24 raw oysters
- 4 lemon crowns, garnish
- 1 Tbsp. parsley, chopped, garnish
- 24 chilled shot glasses

Oysters in Champagne Sauce

SERVES 4
PREPARATION TIME:
30 MINUTES
COOKING TIME:
15 MINUTES

12 fresh oysters in the shell

⅓ cup oyster liquor or fish stock

¼ cup champagne

1 tsp. shallot, minced

¼ cup heavy cream

2 egg yolks

2 tsps. lemon juice

¼ tsp. salt

¼ tsp. white pepper

½ cup unsalted butter

3 cups rock salt

¼ cup Parmesan cheese, freshly grated

OPEN THE OYSTERS over a bowl in order to save the liquor contained within the shells. Discard the top or flat half of the shell. Strain the accumulated oyster liquor through wet cheesecloth or a paper coffee filter to remove dirt or shell particles that may be present. Place the liquor, champagne and shallots in a non-aluminum saucepan and cook until the liquid is reduced to ¼ cup. Add the heavy cream and reduce again until only ¼ cup of liquid remains.

Cook the oysters in a 350° oven on a sheet pan for 2 minutes or until the edges of the oysters just begin to curl. Do not overcook! Pour off any liquid that collects in the oyster shells and reserve.

In the bowl of a food processor or blender place the egg yolks, lemon juice, salt and pepper. Melt the butter in a small pan until it is sizzling hot, and with the machine running, pour in the butter in a slow, steady stream. Then slowly add the champagne reduction and any reserved oyster liquor you may have.

Place the oysters on a layer of rock salt on a sheet pan and cover each mollusk with some of the champagne sauce. The rock salt is used to form a bed for the oysters. If you have no rock salt, you might improvise with balls of aluminum foil to keep the oysters from tipping over.

Sprinkle with the Parmesan cheese, then broil until the sauce is bubbly and browned. Serve 3 oysters per person.

Peppered Halibut Gravlax with Vodka

SERVES 4
PREPARATION TIME:
10 MINUTES
(NOTE MARINATING TIME)

Clean and rinse halibut, leaving the skin on.
Mix together the sugar, salt and cracked black pepper.
Sprinkle this mixture liberally along the entire length of the halibut.

Sprinkle the jalapeño, mixed peppers and chili flakes over halibut, then pour the vodka over the fish. Cover and place weight on top of the halibut and leave to marinate for a minimum of 48 hours in the refrigerator.

Before serving, slice halibut into pieces of desired thickness.

1 side halibut, skin on

1 Tbsp. sugar

1 Tbsp. rock salt

1 Tbsp. black pepper, cracked

6 jalapeño peppers, finely diced

1 red pepper, finely diced

1 green pepper, finely diced

1 yellow pepper, finely diced

Chile flakes to taste

⅓ cup vodka

Pesto and Prosciutto Palmiers

YIELD: 24
PREPARATION TIME:
15 MINUTES
(NOTE REFRIGERATION
TIME)
BAKING TIME:
15 MINUTES
PREHEAT OVEN TO 425°

Palmiers

1 box Pepperidge
    Farm frozen puff
    pastry

¼ lb. thinly sliced
    prosciutto

⅔ cup pesto

¼ cup freshly grated
    Parmesan cheese

Pesto

YIELD: 2 CUPS
PREPARATION TIME:
15 MINUTES

4 garlic cloves

2 cups fresh basil
    leaves, packed

⅔ cup fresh parsley

¼ cup pine nuts or
    walnuts

½ cup olive oil

¾ cup freshly grated
    Parmesan cheese

DEFROST THE PUFF PASTRY SHEETS per package directions. Lightly flour a clean work surface and roll the pastry to make the sheets slightly thinner. Arrange a single layer of prosciutto on each of the sheets, leaving a ¾-inch border of pastry. Divide the pesto and spread atop the ham. Sprinkle with the Parmesan cheese.

Arrange the puff pastry so that the short edges are at the top and bottom. Fold the short sides in to the middle so that the edges meet in the center of the pastry. Fold each of these halves again so that the rolled edges meet in the middle. Now, fold these two sides together so that you have one long strip, six layers thick. Trim the ends off the pastry and then cut into ½-inch slices. Place on a buttered or parchment-lined baking sheet, spacing the slices at least 2 inches apart so they have room to spread. Cover the tray with plastic wrap and chill the palmiers for 30 minutes.

Bake in the middle of the oven for 12 to 15 minutes or until the palmiers are puffed, golden and crisp. Cool for a few minutes, then transfer to a wire rack. Serve hot or cold.

Pesto

In a blender or food processor purée the garlic, basil, parsley and pine nuts. When smooth, add the olive oil and process again briefly. Stir in the Parmesan and season to taste. If the pesto is very stiff or dry, add more olive oil.

Pot Stickers with Lobster in Three Dipping Sauces

Cut the vegetables and mushrooms into 1-inch pieces and place in a food processor. Process until finely chopped. Place the chopped vegetables in a large bowl and add the garlic, ginger, sesame oil, rice wine vinegar, salt, soy sauce and chili oil. Check the seasonings and add more vinegar and salt if the filling tastes flat. Add the chopped lobster meat.

Place a wrapper on a flat work surface and place 1 heaping

teaspoon of the vegetable filling in the middle of the wrapper. Moisten the entire edge of the wrapper by dipping your finger in a cup of cool water, then gently rubbing around the edge of the wrapper. Crimp from one side to the other in even folds, completely sealing the dumpling. Repeat process until you have made enough for 5 for each person or as many as desired.

Heat 1 Tbsp. vegetable oil in a sauté pan or wok until very hot. Cook pot stickers for 30 seconds until light golden, then reduce heat to medium. Pour in about ¼ cup water and cover. Cook the dumplings for another minute, remove cover and serve at once.

Serve with the dipping sauces of soy sauce, rice wine vinegar and Chinese chili paste.

SERVES 4
PREPARATION TIME:
1 HOUR

- 1 **carrot**
- 4 **scallions**
- ¼ **head red cabbage**
- ¼ **head green cabbage**
- 4 **shiitake mushrooms**
- 1 **oz. dried tree ear mushrooms**
- 1 **garlic clove, minced**
- 2 **tsps. fresh ginger, very finely chopped**
- 2 **Tbsps. sesame oil**
- ¼ **cup rice wine vinegar**
- 1 **tsp. salt**
- 1 **Tbsp. soy sauce**
- 1 **tsp. chili oil**
- 1¼ **lbs. lobster, cooked and picked**
- 1 **package round pot sticker wrappers or wonton wrappers**
- 1 **Tbsp. vegetable oil**
  Soy sauce for dipping
  Rice wine vinegar for dipping
  Chinese chili paste for dipping

Ricotta Cheese and Figs in Grape Leaves

SERVES 4

PREPARATION TIME:

25 MINUTES

PREHEAT OVEN TO 350°

¼ lb. figs, fresh or
dried

½ cup cream

1 egg

½ lb. ricotta cheese

4 Tbsps. pine nuts,
toasted

2 Tbsps. chives,
chopped

Grape leaves

IN A FOOD PROCESSOR, purée the figs with cream. Remove and place in a mixing bowl. Whisk in the egg and ricotta cheese. Fold in the pine nuts and chives.

Wrap a teaspoon of filling in each individual grape leaf.

Place on a sheet pan or cookie pan lined with parchment paper in 350° oven and bake until warm, about 15 minutes.

Allow to cool slightly before serving.

COOKING SECRET

Fresh grape leaves may be used, but they need to be boiled for 1½ hours in salt water and marinated in   live oil prior to using.

Rock Shrimp and Mango with Coconut Milk Curry

PEEL MANGOES and pare away the flesh in broad, thin slices. Arrange slices on a plate or tray, season with ground black pepper and sprinkle liberally with sugar.

In a small saucepan, melt the butter and add the shallot and garlic. Cook gently for 1 to 2 minutes. Mix the flour and curry powder together. Stir into the shallot mixture and add the white wine.

Open the can of coconut milk. Pour off some of the clear liquid and reserve. Add the rest to the curry and stir well. Bring to a boil and cook until the liquid is reduced by approximately half. Add the lemon juice and season to taste. Set aside.

Sauté the shrimp in a large skillet with the clarified butter. When the shrimp lose their translucence, add the curry sauce and mix well together. Season if necessary. If sauce is too thick, add a little of the reserved coconut liquid.

Arrange the mango slices on plate in a flower pattern. Put the curried shrimp in the center and sprinkle with chopped chives. Garnish with chive flowers.

SERVES 4
PREPARATION TIME:
45 MINUTES

- 2 **mangoes**
  Ground black pepper
  Granulated sugar
- 2 **Tbsps. butter**
- 1 **shallot, chopped fine**
- 1 **garlic clove, chopped fine**
- 1 **tsp. flour**
- 1 **Tbsp. curry powder**
- 1 **Tbsp. white wine**
- 1 **14 oz. can Thai coconut milk**
- ½ **Tbsp. lemon juice**
  Salt and pepper to taste
- ½ **lb. fresh rock shrimp, peeled and deveined**
- 2 **Tbsps. clarified butter**
  Chives and chive flowers for garnish

Rotolo di Prosciutto and Formaggi

SERVES 8
PREPARATION TIME:
1 HOUR
(NOTE REFRIGERATION TIME)

1¼ lbs. mozzarella cheese, sliced

¾ lb. fontina cheese

Freshly ground black pepper

⅓ lb. prosciutto ham, sliced paper-thin

3 small zucchini

1 bunch fresh basil

Tomato-Basil Vinaigrette
YIELD: 3 CUPS
PREPARATION TIME:
30 MINUTES

2 Tbsps. balsamic vinegar

1 shallot, minced

2 garlic cloves, minced

½ cup extra-virgin olive oil

5 ripe tomatoes, peeled, seeded and diced

25 fresh basil leaves, shredded

Salt and fresh ground pepper to taste

For the Rotolo: Place a double thickness of damp cheesecloth or a linen towel on a clean counter surface. Arrange the mozzarella slices on the cloth, overlapping the edges slightly to form a solid rectangle approximately 7 inches wide by 27 inches long.

Slice the fontina cheese and place it on an ovenproof plate. Melt the cheese in a microwave or conventional oven until it is soft and creamy.

Working quickly, spread the melted fontina over the mozzarella layer, taking care to cover the overlapping edges of the cheese slices. Generously grind fresh pepper over the entire surface.

Next, arrange half of the prosciutto ham in a single layer over the cheese.

Using a vegetable peeler, slice the zucchini lengthwise into very thin strips. Cover the ham with the zucchini, then top with a layer of basil leaves.

Cover the surface with the remaining prosciutto and then roll up the entire ensemble as tightly as possible, starting at the narrow, short end.

Wrap the Rotolo in the cheesecloth or towel and refrigerate overnight. Slice with a serrated knife and serve at room temperature on a pool of Tomato-Basil Vinaigrette.

Tomato-Basil Vinaigrette

Combine the vinegar, shallot and garlic in a bowl and whisk in the olive oil. Add the tomatoes and basil and stir to combine.

Season to taste with salt and pepper. If necessary, add 1 tsp. of sugar to balance the acidity.

Rouge et Noir Brie Quiche

PLACE THE BRIE CHEESE and half and half in a blender and process until smooth. Add salt, white pepper and nutmeg, and process. Quickly add the egg yolks, eggs and chives. Do not overwork. Then add the heavy cream.

When it is well mixed, pour the liquid into the prebaked pie shell and put the quiche in the middle of the 350° oven. Let it bake slowly for 45 to 55 minutes. This quiche will have a different texture than a regular quiche. If it browns too rapidly, cover with foil and lower the temperature.

YIELD:
ONE 8-INCH PIE
PREPARATION TIME:
20 MINUTES
PREHEAT OVEN TO 350°

6 oz. Brie cheese

¾ cup half and half

  Salt and white pepper to taste

  Pinch of nutmeg

3 egg yolks

2 whole eggs

2 tsps. chives, finely chopped

¾ cup heavy cream

1 prebaked 8-inch pie shell

Samoosas

YIELD:
3 TO 4 DOZEN
PREPARATION TIME:
1½ HOURS
(NOTE REFRIGERATION
TIME)

Filling

1 **Tbsp. vegetable oil**

1 **cup finely minced onion**

2 **Tbsps. grated fresh ginger root**

3 **garlic cloves, minced**

1 **lb. ground beef**

½ **tsp. cayenne pepper**

½ **tsp. ground cardamom**

¼ **tsp. cinnamon**

2 **tsps. curry powder, or more to taste**

1 **tsp. salt**

¼ **tsp. ground cloves**

½ **tsp. ground cumin**

½ **tsp. ground coriander**

Juice of half a lemon

1 **Tbsp. finely diced dried apricot**

2 **Tbsps. golden raisins**

Heat the oil in a large skillet and sauté the onion, ginger root and garlic over moderate heat for 4 or 5 minutes.

Add the remaining filling ingredients and cook for 10 minutes or so, or until the beef is cooked. Drain off any excess fat and set the mixture aside to cool. Taste and adjust seasonings if desired.

To make the pastry, place the flour and salt in the bowl of a food processor and pulse to blend. Add the shortening and mix thoroughly. With the machine running, add about ½ cup of ice water and pulse to incorporate. Check the consistency of the dough and add more water by the teaspoon until the pastry just holds together when you pinch a bit between your fingers. Transfer the dough to a floured surface and divide it into four pieces, flattening each one into a patty. Cover with plastic wrap and refrigerate 1 hour. If you do not have a food processor, make the pastry in a bowl, following the same basic procedure; use two knives or a pastry blender to cut the shortening into the flour mixture.

To form the samoosas, roll one of the pastry disks into a thin sheet. Use a 4-inch circular ring to cut out as many rounds as possible from the dough.

Place a dollop of meat filling on one half of each circle, brush the edge of the pastry with water and then fold in half to make a crescent shape. Do not overfill the samoosas or they will split apart during the frying stage. Crimp together the edges of the dough with a fork. Repeat with all of the remaining pastry dough and filling. Please note: if you are using egg roll wrappers instead of the traditional pastry, cut the sheets in half and make triangular-shaped samoosas. Use water to seal the edges; crimping is not necessary.

At this stage the samoosas can be frozen for several months if desired. Arrange them on sheet trays so they do not touch and freeze until solid. Then, bag or store them in an airtight container. Do not defrost before cooking.

To cook, heat enough oil in a skillet or saucepan to deep fry the samoosas. You will need oil to a depth of at least 1 inch. Bring the temperature of the oil to 375°, then fry the samoosas in small batches until golden brown. Drain on paper towels and serve hot or at room temperature.

Pastry

4 cups flour

1½ tsps. salt

1⅓ cups solid shortening

⅔ cup ice water

4 cups vegetable oil for frying

Satay Sticks

YIELD:
12 TO 16 SKEWERS
PREPARATION TIME:
30 MINUTES
(NOTE MARINATING TIME)

Coconut Milk
YIELD: 2 CUPS
PREPARATION TIME:
5 MINUTES
(NOTE COOLING TIME)
COOKING TIME:
20 MINUTES
PREHEAT OVEN TO 400°

1 **large coconut**

2 **cups boiling water**

Satay Sticks

1 **lb. boneless chicken breast or tenderloin of beef or pork**

2 **Tbsps. curry powder**

½ **tsp. salt**

1 **Tbsp. ground coriander**

1 **Tbsp. sugar**

1 **cup coconut milk**

½ **cup peanut oil**

1 **Tbsp. rice wine vinegar**

FOR THE COCONUT MILK, find an ice pick or screwdriver, and with a hammer, pierce a hole in one of the eyes of the coconut so that you can discard the coconut water. Place the coconut on a baking tray and bake at 400° for 15 to 20 minutes or until the shell cracks. Remove the nut from the oven and let it cool before further handling.

Wrap the coconut in a towel and smash it into several pieces with a mallet or hammer. Peel off the brown skin with a vegetable peeler and then cut the coconut into small pieces. Place the coconut meat in a blender or food processor and pour in the boiling water. Process until the meat is finely chopped.

Transfer the contents of the food processor to a sieve and strain the liquid into a large bowl. Wrap the coconut meat in a clean linen towel and firmly squeeze any remaining milk into the bowl. Refrigerate the coconut milk if you are not using it right away, as it does not keep well.

Satay Sticks

Cut meat into strips 1 inch wide by 2 inches long by ³⁄₁₆ inch thick.

Thread the meat onto bamboo skewers so that no wood is visible except at the handle end. Do not crowd or ribbon the meat or it will not cook properly.

Mix the curry, salt, coriander and sugar together and coat the meat with this seasoning. Let the meat rest for 10 minutes.

Add the liquid ingredients to the meat, mix well and marinate at room temperature for 1 hour.

Barbecue the filled skewers until they are cooked through, turning only once.

Serve the satay sticks with Peanut Sauce and Cucumber Condiment.

Peanut Sauce

Combine the ingredients in a pan and simmer over low heat until the sauce thickens.

Cucumber Condiment

Combine ingredients, garnish with chopped peanuts and chill.

Peanut Sauce

½ tsp. Tabasco

1 Tbsp. curry powder

2 Tbsps. sugar

3 Tbsps. chunky peanut butter

1 cup coconut milk

Cucumber Condiment

1 cup very thinly sliced English cucumber

1 Tbsp. water

2 tsps. rice wine vinegar

¼ tsp. Tabasco

½ tsp. salt

1 Tbsp. chopped peanuts for garnish

Seared Scallop and Duck Foie Gras on Caramelized Pineapple

SERVES 8
PREPARATION TIME:
35 MINUTES

1 fresh pineapple

1 Tbsp. ginger, pickled

2 Tbsps. sake

2 Tbsps. mirin*

1 vanilla bean

⅓ cup rice wine vinegar

¾ cup olive oil

Salt and pepper to taste

1 lb. scallops

16 oz. duck foie gras

8 leaves bok choy

1 bunch cilantro for garnish

Slice pineapple into 8 1½ inch thick rounds. Place remaining pineapple in a saucepan with ginger. Add sake and mirin.

Cut vanilla bean in half and scrape. Add to the saucepan and simmer for 10 to 12 minutes. Cool and remove the vanilla bean in discard. Place mixture in a blender and blend with the rice wine vinegar. Slowly add olive oil and season to taste.

In a very hot pan, put 1 Tbsp. olive oil and scallops. Sauté. Add pineapple and cook for 1 to 2 minutes. Remove and add foie gras. Cook quickly on both sides.

Heat bok choy. Season to taste with salt and pepper.

Place boy choy on pineapple slices. Top with scallops and foie gras. Lightly top with pineapple vinaigrette and garnish with cilantro.

Mirin is a low-alcohol, sweet golden wine made from glutinous rice.

Shrimp with Prosciutto di Parma

WRAP EACH SHRIMP with a half slice of prosciutto. Sauté the wrapped shrimp in the butter until the prosciutto is slightly browned. Add the Grand Marnier and the orange juice.

Cook for about 3 minutes or until the liquid transforms into a glaze. Season to taste with pepper.

SERVES 4
PREPARATION TIME:
15 MINUTES

12 **large shrimp, shelled and deveined**

6 **slices Prosciutto di Parma, sliced in half**

3 **Tbsps. sweet butter**

¼ **cup Grand Marnier**

Juice of 3 fresh oranges

Ground black pepper to taste

Skillet-Roasted Mussels Flamed in Lemon-Anise Infused Vodka

SERVES 2
PREPARATION TIME:
15 MINUTES
(NOTE INFUSING TIME FOR VODKA)

1 **lb. mussels**

¾ **oz. Lemon-Anise Infused Vodka (recipe follows)**

Sea salt to taste

Black pepper to taste

Lemon-Anise Infused Vodka
YIELD: 2 CUPS
PREPARATION TIME:
5 MINUTES
(NOTE INFUSING TIME)

2 **cups vodka**

1 **lemon, peeled and quartered**

½ **tsp. anise seed**

PLACE MUSSELS in a container and cover with cold water. One by one, remove the mussels from the water. Throw out any open mussels. Remove beards and dirt. Place in dry container and keep cold until ready to use. Bring a large cast-iron skillet to near smoking over high heat. Add the mussels in a single layer. Shake the pan every few seconds. As soon as the mussels open, season with sea salt and black pepper. Sprinkle on the infused vodka. Let flame—stand back—and then slide the mussels into a large bowl.

Serve with lemon wedges.

Lemon-Anise Infused Vodka

In a clean glass container, place all ingredients and let infuse for 5 days.

Small Red Potatoes Stuffed with Smoked Trout Mousse and Caviar

Boil potatoes in salted water until soft. Plunge immediately into ice water. When cold, remove and pat dry.

Cut in half and cut a small slice off the bottom of each piece so they sit nicely on a plate. Scoop out a small amount of potato with a melon baller. Sprinkle potatoes with salt and pepper and set aside.

In a food processor, soften cream cheese. Add trout, horseradish, dill, salt, pepper and lemon juice. Place the resulting mousse in a pastry bag fitted with fluted tip and pipe onto the potatoes. Garnish with a small amount of caviar and a dill sprig.

SERVES 4
PREPARATION TIME:
45 MINUTES

12 egg-sized red potatoes

½ cup cream cheese

1 side smoked trout

1 Tbsp. prepared horseradish

1 tsp. dill, chopped

Salt and pepper to taste

Squeeze of lemon juice

2 Tbsps. American caviar

Dill sprigs for garnish

Smoked Salmon

SERVES 2

**PREPARATION TIME:
20 MINUTES**

4 **chive crepes**

4 **oz. smoked salmon,
thinly sliced**

1 **oz. onion, finely
diced**

2 **tsps. chives, finely
diced**

1 **hard boiled egg,
chopped**

Zest from 1 lemon

**Pink peppercorns
for garnish**

**Crème fraîche for
garnish**

WARM CREPES and place one on each plate. Shingle half the smoked salmon to cover the center of the crepe.

Sprinkle with onions, chives, egg and lemon zest.

Fold a second crepe in half and place on top of the salmon and condiments.

Drizzle with crème fraîche and sprinkle with pink peppercorns.

Smoked Salmon Pinwheels

FOR THE FILLING, blend the cream cheese with the onion, horseradish and dill. Add a few grinds of black pepper and salt to taste.

Lay out the smoked salmon slices on the paper to form a rectangle approximately 7 × 14-inches. Cover it with another sheet of paper or plastic wrap. Roll gently with a rolling pin to make a nice thin, even layer.

Take off the top paper and spread the cream cheese filling evenly over the salmon. Use the paper to help roll up the salmon, jelly roll fashion. Wrap it up in the paper and place in the freezer to chill well for about 30 minutes.

Cut the roll into even slices, approximately ¼-inch thick, and place them on cucumber slices, or crackers if you prefer. Garnish with dill sprigs.

COOKING SECRET

For variations, try adding capers, parsley, chives, wasabi, pickles, anchovy, lemon juice, brandy, mustard or sugar to the cream cheese mixture.

SERVES 4
PREPARATION TIME:
30 MINUTES
(NOTE REFRIGERATION
TIME)

1 **lb. cream cheese, softened**

2 **Tbsps. red onion, chopped**

2 **Tbsps. horseradish**

1 **Tbsp. fresh dill, chopped**

Ground black pepper and salt to taste

¾ **lb. thin–sliced smoked salmon (lox)**

1 **English cucumber, sliced**

Dill sprigs for garnish

Parchment or waxed paper.

Smoked Trout Sandwich with Lemon Dill Mayonnaise

SERVES 4

PREPARATION TIME:
25 MINUTES

¼ **cup sour cream**

¼ **cup mayonnaise**

Zest of 1 lemon

Chopped fresh dill to taste

Salt and pepper to taste

4 **slices pumpernickel bread**

Watercress leaves

1 **cucumber, thinly sliced**

2 **smoked trout fillets**

2 **sliced quail eggs (optional)**

Chopped fresh dill

IN A MIXING BOWL combine the sour cream, mayonnaise, lemon zest, dill, salt and pepper. Set aside.

Toast pumpernickel bread and spread with lemon dill mayonnaise. Layer first with watercress, then cucumber, then with trout.

Dot trout with a touch of lemon dill mayonnaise, top with sliced quail egg and chopped dill.

Spicy Orange Shrimp

COMBINE ALL of the marinade ingredients in a small bowl and whisk to blend.

Add the shrimp and stir, cover with plastic wrap and refrigerate at least 4 hours before cooking.

When ready to serve, heat your barbecue, adjusting the rack about two inches above the coals. Grill over a medium to high heat. The marinade is sweet, so it will burn if you are not careful. Shrimp cook quickly—5 to 7 minutes should be sufficient.

SERVES 6
PREPARATION TIME:
15 MINUTES
(NOTE MARINATING TIME)

½ **cup frozen orange juice concentrate**

¼ **cup peanut oil**

¼ **cup soy sauce**

2 **Tbsps. white wine**

2 **Tbsps. sweet hot mustard**

2 **tsps. sesame oil**

2 **tsps. five-spice powder**

1 **garlic clove, minced**

1 **lb. large raw shrimp, peeled and deveined**

Spring Roll with Beet Vinaigrette

YIELD:
4 SPRING ROLLS
PREPARATION TIME:
45 MINUTES
(NOTE MARINATING TIME)

1 tsp. fresh ginger, chopped

1 tsp. fresh garlic, chopped

4 scallions, chopped

4 shiitake mushrooms, stems discarded, caps into thin strips

1 carrot, julienned

2 fennel bulbs, sliced thin

¼ cup cilantro, chopped

2 Tbsps. sesame oil

Salt to taste

½ lb. salmon, grilled rare

4 egg roll wrappers

Peanut oil for frying

Vinaigrette

5 medium beets

1 Tbsp. lime juice

¼ cup light vegetable oil or olive oil

1 Tbsp. cilantro, chopped

1 Tbsp. shallots, chopped

½ tsp. garlic, chopped

Heat the sesame oil over medium heat. Add the ginger, garlic, scallions and mushrooms. Cook for 2 minutes. Add the fennel and carrot. Cook for 2 to 3 minutes. Remove from heat and season with salt and cilantro. Cool.

Slice the grilled, rare salmon into 4 equal pieces.

Lay the egg roll skins flat on table. Fill each with ¼ cup of the fennel mixture.

Top with 1 piece of salmon.

Top with another ¼ cup of the fennel mixture. Roll up and seal edges by dampening your finger in water.

Deep fry in peanut oil at 350° for 6 to 8 minutes.

Vinaigrette

Peel, chop and purée the beets in a blender. You should have about 1 cup. Place in a saucepan and cook until you have ½ cup left.

Add the remaining ingredients and let stand at room temperature at least 1 hour before serving.

To serve, place ¼ cup of the beet vinaigrette on each serving plate. Cut the ends off the spring rolls and then slice into 2 pieces on a large bias. Stand spring rolls on end.

COOKING SECRET

For a spicy vinaigrette, add two dashes of Tabasco sauce.

Stuffed Morels

Remove the morel stems and chop them.

Make the risotto by gently sautéing the shallot, garlic and rice in the olive oil. Add 3 cups of the stock, a cupful at a time, and the mushroom chopped stems and cook over moderate heat until the rice is tender and the liquid is absorbed. Season to taste and add the cream and cheese.

With a pastry bag and a plain tube, pipe the risotto into the morels. Do not overstuff. A hint for stuffing is to make a tiny incision in the closed end to allow air to escape.

Season the mushrooms with salt and pepper and sauté them in a little oil in a covered skillet for 4 to 5 minutes on each side.

Remove the mushrooms and keep them warm. Discard the cooking oil. Deglaze the skillet with the vinegar and the remaining ½ cup of stock. Add the pine nuts and sun-dried tomatoes. Cook gently for 1 minute. Add the basil and extra-virgin olive oil.

Toss the greens with this mixture and dish up with the mushrooms on top. Add some shaved Parmesan to taste.

SERVES 4
PREPARATION TIME:
45 MINUTES

- 8 large morels
- 1 Tbsp. shallot, chopped
- ½ tsp. garlic, chopped
- ⅔ cup Arborio rice
- 1 Tbsp. olive oil
- 3½ cups vegetable or chicken stock
- Salt and pepper to taste
- 2 Tbsps. heavy cream, optional
- 2 Tbsps. Parmesan cheese, grated
- Oil for cooking
- 1 Tbsp. balsamic vinegar
- 2 Tbsps. pine nuts
- 2 Tbsps. sun-dried tomatoes
- 2 Tbsps. basil leaves, shredded
- 2 Tbsps. extra-virgin olive oil
- 1 lb. salad greens
- Parmesan cheese to taste

Tapenade

SERVES 4

PREPARATION TIME:

5 MINUTES

½ **cup olives, pitted and rinsed**

1 **Tbsp. capers, rinsed**

2 **tsps. Dijon mustard**

2 **Tbsps. water**

¼ **cup olive oil**

PLACE THE first four ingredients in a blender or food processor and pulse until coarsely chopped.

With the machine running, drizzle in the olive oil and purée until not quite smooth.

Serve on crackers or toast rounds.

Tender Corn Pancake with Salmon and Golden Caviar

PLUNGE HUSKED CORN into boiling, salted water for 8 minutes, then quickly remove the corn and plunge into ice water. When completely cooled, cut the corn off the cob and mix in a blender with the egg and flour. Adjust seasoning.

Cut 6 small, thin slices of salmon and season each piece. Place a small tsp. of caviar in the middle of each piece. Fold the sides of the salmon inward. Place 2 Tbsps. of the corn mixture in a greased or Teflon pan and top with salmon. Put an additional Tbsp. of the corn mixture on top of the salmon and cook for approximately 5 minutes on each side.

Garnish with sour cream, golden caviar and chopped chives.

SERVES 4
PREPARATION TIME:
30 MINUTES

12 oz. corn on the
   cob, blanched

 3 eggs

 2 oz. flour

   Salt and pepper to
   taste

10 to 12 oz. salmon,
   uncooked

 2 oz. golden caviar

Thai Crab Cakes

SERVES 4
PREPARATION TIME:
15 MINUTES

2 **cups crab meat**

2 **cups panco (Japanese bread crumbs)**

1 **cup mayonnaise**

½ **bunch green onions, chopped fine**

2 **Tbsps. basil, chopped fine**

2 **Tbsps. cilantro, chopped fine**

2 **Tbsps. mint, chopped fine**

　Fish sauce to taste

1 **Tbsp. olive oil**

IN A LARGE MIXING BOWL combine the crab meat, bread crumbs, mayonnaise, green onions, basil, cilantro, mint and fish sauce to taste. Form mixture together into 2 oz. cakes.

Brown in sauté pan in olive oil for 3 minutes on each side over medium heat or until cooked through.

Thin-Sliced Salmon Baked in a Tender Corn Pancake with Watercress Sauce

SERVES 4
PREPARATION TIME:
45 MINUTES

3 to 4 tender ears of corn

3 whole eggs

2 Tbsps. flour

Salt and pepper to taste

1 small bunch watercress

2 tsps. olive oil

1 Tbsp. shallots, finely chopped

4 Tbsps. dry white wine

¼ cup water

¼ cup cream

½ lb. salmon fillet

4 Tbsps. caviar (white fish, salmon or sturgeon)

18 asparagus tips, cooked

2 tsps. sour cream

1 Tbsp. chives, finely chopped

For the BATTER, peel the husks and silk from the corn. Bring 4 qts. of salted water to a boil. Add the corn and boil for 8 minutes, then quickly dip in cold water. Cut the kernels from the cobs. There should be about 1½ cups of cut corn. In a food processor, place the corn, eggs, flour, salt and pepper. Mix quickly by pulsing, in order to keep the texture of the batter lightly chunky. Check seasoning and pour the batter into a small mixing bowl.

Wash the watercress and trim, discarding the stems. Cook the leaves in a pot of boiling, salted water until just tender, about 3 minutes. Drain in a strainer. Refresh the leaves under cold running water, then squeeze all the moisture from the watercress, using your hands. In a small sauce pot, heat 1 tsp. of olive oil. Add the chopped shallots and sauté until they are a light golden color. Deglaze with the white wine and reduce to almost dry. Add the water and the cream, bringing mixture to a boil. Add the cooked watercress leaves. Run the mixture through a blender 2 to 3 minutes until you obtain a light, bright green and very tasty watercress sauce. Check the seasoning.

Slice evenly and thinly 6 scaloppines of salmon, by holding a very sharp knife at a 30° angle. On a plate, spread them out and top each scaloppine with one teaspoon of caviar. Fold over the scaloppine so that the caviar is sealed between the two layers of salmon. Season the salmon with salt and pepper on both sides.

Grease a sauté pan with the remaining teaspoon of olive oil. Put in 1½ Tbsps. of the corn pancake mixture and cook in a minute. Top the mixture with the scaloppine of salmon and barely cover the salmon with another thin layer of corn mixture. Cook 4 to 6 pancakes at a time, turning once. Cook until golden brown on one side, turn and cook until golden brown on the other side.

When the pancakes are cooked, cover the center of each warm plate with watercress sauce. Display a pancake in the center of each plate and garnish them attractively with the cooked asparagus tips. Top each pancake with ½ tsp. sour cream and the remaining caviar. Sprinkle with chopped chives.

Tipsy Hood Canal Clams

COMBINE ALL INGREDIENTS except paprika in a large kettle or pot. Steam until the clams are open and done. Garnish with paprika before serving.

SERVES 4
PREPARATION TIME:
30 MINUTES

20 steamer clams, small to medium size

½ bottle of Chardonnay

½ cup butter or margarine

4 cups bread crumbs

1½ tsps. Worcestershire sauce

2 tsps. garlic, finely minced

1 tsp. dry mustard

¼ tsp. Tabasco sauce

¼ cup parsley, chopped

Paprika for garnish

Vegetable Spring Rolls

SERVES 6
PREPARATION TIME:
45 MINUTES

Oil

2 Tbsps. ginger, minced

1 Tbsp. garlic, minced

½ cup scallions, thinly sliced

3 small serrano chiles

2 cups diced onion

1½ cups diced celery

1½ cups shredded carrots

6 cups diced Napa cabbage

1¼ cups rice noodles (soaked)

2½ Tbsps. salt

2½ Tbsps. sugar

⅔ cup rice wine vinegar

⅓ cup soy sauce

2 Tbsps. cornstarch

3 Tbsps. water

Rice paper wrappers or vegetable wraps: romaine lettuce, grape leaves or spinach

Three-chile dipping sauce (recipe follows)

Heat oil in a wok and add the ginger, garlic, scallions and serrano chiles. Add the onions and let sweat for 3 minutes. Add the celery, carrots and Napa cabbage and sauté 3 minutes. Add the drained noodles and mix in well. Stir in the salt, sugar, rice wine vinegar and soy sauce.

In a small mixing bowl combine the cornstarch with the water and add to the vegetable mixture. Stir until the filling turns heavy and glossy. Remove from heat and allow mixture to cool.

Place ⅓ cup of the filling diagonally across the lower third of the wrapper. Bring the tip of the lower corner over the filling and roll once. Bring the left and right flaps together and wet each tip to seal. Roll tightly. Seal the last tip.

Sauté in oil, turning constantly, until golden brown and crisp, about 4 to 5 minutes. if you are using leaf wrappers, spray a skillet or wok with vegetable oil and stir-fry for 2 to 3 minutes.

Three-chile dipping sauce

6 garlic cloves

¼ cup sugar

3 chiles of choice: Anaheim, poblano, habañero, jalapeño, pasilla

Juice of 2 limes

½ cup fish sauce

1 cup water

1 tsp. rice vinegar

Combine the garlic cloves, sugar, chiles and lime juice in a food processor. Process until smooth. Add remaining ingredients and pulse until blended.

Wild Mushroom Crostini

SERVES 4
PREPARATION TIME:
30 MINUTES

In a large sauté pan, heat the butter over medium-high heat. Add the garlic and the mushrooms and sauté until the mushroom liquid has evaporated. Add the white wine, reduce the heat and simmer until nearly all the liquid has evaporated. Remove from heat and season, setting aside until ready to use.

To serve, spread the mushroom mixture on slices of baguette. Arrange on a plate, sprinkle with the chives and toasted hazelnuts and serve.

- 1 Tbsp. clarified butter
- 2 garlic cloves, peeled and minced
- ¾ lb. wild or button mushrooms, stemmed, cleaned and chopped
- ¼ cup white wine
  Salt and pepper to taste
- 1 baguette, sliced on the bias into ½-inch pieces, toasted
  Minced chives for garnish
  Toasted hazelnuts for garnish, chopped

Wild Mushroom Quesadilla with Herbed Cheese

SERVES 4
PREPARATION TIME:
15 MINUTES
PREHEAT OVEN TO 350°

¼ **cup portobello mushrooms**

¼ **cup oyster mushrooms**

¼ **cup shiitake mushrooms**

¼ **cup black trumpet mushrooms**

¼ **cup chanterelles**

2 **Tbsps. truffle oil**

1 **tsp. thyme, chopped**

1 **tsp. rosemary, chopped**

1 **tsp. roasted garlic, chopped**

1 **Tbsp. shallots, chopped**

3 **oz. Boursine cheese**

8 **flour tortilla**

CLEAN ALL THE MUSHROOMS with a damp cloth. Remove the stems from the oyster mushrooms. Cut the black trumpet mushrooms lengthwise in half. Mix the cleaned mushrooms with the truffle oil the chopped herbs as well as with the chopped garlic and shallots. Place in a large ovenproof pan and spread out over the entire surface of the pan. Bake in the oven at 350° until soft.

Remove the mushrooms from the pan and place in a steel mixing bowl. Mix the cheese in thoroughly while the mushrooms are still warm.

Spread ¼ of the mixture over a tortilla, covering the entire surface, then cover with another and brown under a broiler until the cheese is melted and the tortilla is crispy.

Won Ton Stuffed With Shrimp, Pork, Water Chestnut and Mushrooms

SOAK THE DRIED MUSHROOMS in hot water for 1 hour. In a large mixing bowl, combine the pork, shrimp, onion, garlic, oyster sauce, pepper, sugar and water chestnuts.

Place 1 heaping Tbsp. of mixture on each won ton wrapper. Fold into a triangle, sealing weges with a moistened finger and deep fry until golden brown.

SERVES 4
PREPARATION TIME:
30 MINUTES
(NOTE SOAKING TIME)

¼ **lb. dried wild mushrooms, finely chopped**

1 **lb. ground pork**

½ **lb. shrimp, diced**

¼ **lb. onion, finely diced**

½ **Tbsp. garlic, chopped**

2 **Tbsps. oyster sauce**

½ **tsp. white pepper**

1½ **Tbsps. sugar**

2 **oz. water chestnuts, diced**

1 **package won ton wrappers**

Oil for frying

Won Ton with Crab Meat and Chives

SERVES 4
PREPARATION TIME:
15 MINUTES

¼ **lb. crab meat**

3 **oz. cream cheese**

3 **drops A-1 sauce**

½ **tsp. salt**

¼ **cup chives,**
   chopped

½ **tsp. black pepper**

¼ **tsp. sesame oil**

16 **won ton skins**

4 **cups vegetable oil**

Plum sauce for
dipping

MIX TOGETHER the crab meat, cream cheese, A-1 sauce, salt, chives, pepper and sesame oil together in a mixing bowl.

Place ½ tsp. of the mixture on each corner of the won ton skin. Fold in half.

Heat oil to 350° and deep fry until the won tons float and turn light brown, less than 1 minute.

Won tons can be served hot or cold. Dip in plum sauce.

Cigars

Cigar Chic

THERE IS AN ART TO THE CIGAR. HOW YOU HOLD IT, STROKE IT, roll it between the thumb and forefinger; how you draw it gently against ready nostrils and take a heady drag off the refined tobacco long before you ever clip off the tip and light business end of the piece.

The whole affair can be quite alluring, really. Particularly if done right. Particularly when paired with a martini. Just ask Bogart or Bacall, Benny or Burns—or anyone who attended the now famous black and white ball of the Dominick Dunnes. It's a good look. And these days, it's all in good taste, if you have a taste for it.

Taste. Chefs and taste experts have spent entire careers endeavoring to match quality cigars with complementary beverages other than the martini. When pairing a cigar with a cocktail, the Manhattan appears to be the marriage of choice. Or is it convenience? According to the elegant consumer who is just chic enough, just daring enough, just I've-got-it-and-I-don't-care-enough to carry it off, it is the martini that knows how to work a smoke-filled room.

Thanks to the likes of Marlon Brando and Al Pacino, the smoke-filled room once connoted power brokering in the context of politics or a consortium of Sicilian dons. Conversely, the cigar itself may evoke the image of an afternoon whiled away in a gentleman's club either now or then, or the bonhomie of a good cigar in the company of a fine port, accompanied by the gentle swish-tock of a grandfather clock in a library of leather-bound classics during the quiet hours of the night. Or, a heady afternoon among women under the guise of high tea...

In a world where image is everything, who were Winston Churchill, Alfred Hitchcock, Groucho Marx or Edward G. Robinson without a cigar? Merely a select, albeit disparate assembly of the famous or notorious who have found solace or satisfaction at the serious end of a stogie—nicknamed, incidentally, after Conestoga, Pennsylvania, one of the earliest towns in America to commercially manufacture cigars.

Ulysses S. Grant counted on an ample supply of cigars to sustain him through every Civil War battle. A century later, President John F. Kennedy made provisions for a supply of more than a thousand Cuban cigars the day before he signed an embargo on Cuban products. And they said the fog disappears before 8 o'clock in Camelot.

Sigmund Freud is said to have attributed his emotional and physical well-being to the consumption of at least 15 cigars a day. Mark Twain, who purportedly smoked 20 a day and invariably sought out the cheapest, worst-smelling stogies he could find, said, "I smoke in moderation; only one cigar at a time." Reports of their innumerable existence surely must have been grossly exaggerated.

Bored with beleaguering advice about what America needed most, Woodrow Wilson's vice president, Thomas Riley Marshall, who otherwise quietly retreated into oblivion, uttered the immortal words, "What this country really needs is a good five-cent cigar." God bless America. And God bless Thomas Riley Marshall.

Novelists William Makepeace Thackeray, Anthony Trollope, Charles Dickens and Evelyn Waugh were cigar aficionados. However, Nobel laureate Rudyard Kipling, in what may go down as the ultimate sexist remark wrote, "A woman's just a woman, but a good cigar's a smoke." Conversely, Mr. Kipling…

In the past, women who smoked cigars were perceived as eccentric or sexually revealing; a woman who smoked a cigar was likely rivaling the male right or role of public pleasure. Amandine Aurore Lucie Dupin or Baroness Dudevant, more commonly known as novelist George Sand and the controversial companion of many, not the least of whom was Frederic Chopin, enjoyed a good cigar as much as a good companion. Bizet's tragic heroine Carmen, worked in a cigar factory and partook of the product long before Madonna ever lit up a

Cigar aficionados know not to inhale the smoke. Instead, savor it in your mouth like fine wine, then release it without swallowing.

double corona on screen. The phenomenon is not new among women; simply unabashed.

The "exclusively male stronghold" of the cigar—viz. Paul Newman, Arnold Schwartzenegger and even Bill Clinton—lost its grasp to such cigar-smoking femmes as Lucille Ball, Bette Midler, Whoopi Goldberg, Sharon Stone, Demi Moore, Ellen Barkin, Jodie Foster and Auntie Joan.

History Goes Up In Smoke

The history of the cigar precedes the evolution of the New World. On October 28, 1492, Columbus landed at the island of Cuba. Columbus historian, Luis de Torres, observed that the natives carried either a lighted piece of coal or rolled tube—*tabaco*—made of cohiba leaves, which they ignited and inhaled. Experts have agreed to disagree on whom they will credit with introducing tobacco to Europe; whether it was Cortez of Spain (1518), Hernandez de Toledo of Portugal, Damien de Goes of the Netherlands or Sir Walter Raleigh of Great Britain. Unquestionably, smoking tobacco had become a popular European habit by the late 16th century and the word *seegar* first appeared in the New English Dictionary in 1735.

The Spanish invented the cigar as we know it today. By 1800, royal cigar factories of Sevilla were flourishing. In 1831, King Ferdinand VII granted Cubans the right to produce and sell tobacco. The Cuban government still sends an annual batch of the best Cuban cigars—Cohibas and Trinidads—to Spanish King Juan Carlos. Spain remains the largest importer of Cuban cigars.

The cigar first became popular in America in 1792, when Revolutionary War hero Israel Putnam introduced the comestible roll to Connecticut, the state, incidentally, which still creates the best cigar wrappers. Cigar smoking in America rose dramatically during the Civil War. Subsequently, many a war was waged by cigar-puffing generals and presidents.

But then a different kind of war broke out and a battle for moderation began. In 1964, the year of the historical "Surgeon General's report" on the potential health effects of tobacco,

Americans were consuming 9 billion cigars, annually. By 1992, that figure had dropped more than 75 percent, to 2 billion a year; less than 100 million of which were imported. Since then, there has been a phenomenal resurgence in the cigar's popularity; not only because it is viewed as the lesser of two evils against the cigarette, but also because of the social status and allure more recently associated with it. Americans are, once again, courting the cigar.

Today, more than 200 million cigars are imported each year, which doesn't include the estimated 6 million cigars that arrive through underground channels from Cuba.

Cigar Legacy

Historically, Cuban cigars have held a corner on the market. Even today, cigars remain a premier cash export for a country otherwise starved for hard currency. The heart of the Cuban cigar industry is the 100,000-acre rich bottom land 100 miles west of Havana, known as the Vuelta Abajo.

During the 120-day growth cycle of the cohiba, each plant is tended by hand more than once a day. When harvested, the tobacco leaves are strung on poles in a barn, where they are left to dry for two months. Once dried, the brown leaves are bunched, flattened, and laid out to ferment naturally, without chemicals, in 100-degree-plus temperatures. After the first fermentation, the leaves are sorted for size, then fermented again. The finest leaves are fermented a third time before being shipped to factories. This ensures a lower level of acidity, tar and nicotine than is found in cigarette tobacco.

The best and most expensive cigars (but by far, the minority), are cut and rolled entirely by hand. The balance of the wrappers are cut with steel oval blades by factory workers, who then press the filler and binders into wooden cigar forms, then wrap and seal the finished cigars.

A good cigar roller makes between 100 and 130 cigars a day, spending 4-5 minutes on each. For more than a century in Cuba, manufacturers have hired people to read aloud to cigar makers during the long work day.

Finished cigars are selected and graded by color so that each cigar box will contain cigars of similar appearance and quality. The final step involves banding and boxing of the product. The finest cigars are reserved for export; the remainder are consumed domestically.

The mass exodus of Cuban cigar makers and the transplantation of Cuban seed throughout the world has effectively destroyed Cuba's monopoly on world-class cigars. For more than a century, Ybor City, near Tampa, Fla., has turned out a superior product. Honduras and the Dominican Republic are world centers of quality production. And the Connecticut shade tobacco leaf is universally in demand as the finest wrapper.

Cigars are made in various sizes, measured by ring gauges based on $\frac{1}{64}$ of an inch. Thus, a gauge of 48 would be $\frac{48}{64}$ of an inch. The larger ring gauge cigars have a fuller taste and a cooler, smoother draw. Moreover, cigars with dark leaf wrappers—*maduros*—have a higher sugar content and are spicy with a sweet taste.

The smallest Havana cigar ever made was the Bolivar Corona Delgado at 1¼ inch; the largest commercial Panatella was more than 19 inches long; and the Koh-l-Noor at 6 feet, was presented to an Indian Maharajah in 1934.

Tips and Technique

Technique is important in many social activities; the cigar is no exception. Always clip or cut the head or closed end of a handmade cigar before lighting. Use a pair of scissors or a cigar guillotine to snip the head about ⅛ of an inch off the top. The cigar label is always closest to the head. The foot is the end of the cigar which is lighted.

Smaller cigars ignite with one match, whereas a larger cigar requires a ritual lighting. Before putting it in your mouth, hold the cigar horizontally in your hand and rotate the foot over a flame until it is burning evenly. Place the cigar in your mouth and lightly draw smoke into your mouth until the tobacco is lit. The cigar should be held firmly between the lips; not clenched between teeth, chewed upon or drooled over. Not even looks warrant a cigar holder; the equivalent of sipping a rare wine through a straw.

Cigar aficionados know not to inhale the smoke. Instead, savor it in your mouth like fine wine, then release it without swallowing. Hold it in the mouth for a few seconds, allowing the tongue and upper palate to savor the aroma. The first half of the cigar always tastes better and is lowest in tar and nicotine. Many practitioners prefer to smoke only the first half or, at most, two-thirds of the cigar.

Fine chefs and taste experts recommend port, wine, brandy or cognac to complement a cigar. The new casual elite are swilling martinis. Beer on a hot day can be refreshing and, if non-alcoholic beverages are in order, espresso or fresh juice seem to work well. Besides, just about anything looks good in a martini glass.

Index of Appetizers

Index of Martinis by Base

Index of Martinis by Ingredients

ROMANA SAMBUCA
Ozzon Martini—Club 36 **103**
Romana Martini—Tongue & Groove **106**

RUM
Jamaican Martini—The Martini Club **114**
Pineapple Rum Martini—The Martini Club **104**

SAKE
Yang Martini—Inagiku **84**
Ying Martini—Inagiku **84**

SCOTCH
Smokey Martini—Pravda **111**

SLOE GIN
Red Gin-Gin—The Mandarin **83**

SWEET AND SOUR MIX
Lemon Drop Martini—Tongue & Groove **99**
Limonnaya Martini—The Martini Club **100**
Razamataz—Club XIX at The Lodge at Pebble Beach **105**
Sweet Cosmopolitan—Tongue & Groove **107**

TRIPLE SEC
Cosmopolitan—Top of the Hub **90**
Kurant Cosmopolitan—Compass Rose **98**
Lemon Cosmopolitan—The Martini Club **99**
Lemon Drop Martini—Tongue & Groove **99**
Park Place Martini—Mumbo Jumbo **82**
Sweet Cosmopolitan—Tongue & Groove **107**

TUACA
Campton Cosmo—Campton Place Hotel **86**
Frangelico Martini—Pravda **94**

VERMOUTH
All Too Important Martini—Johnny Love's **76**
Blue Sapphire—The Mandarin **76**
Classic Dry—The Martini Club **77**
Classic Old Fashioned Martini—The Lenox Room **77**
Classic Sapphire—The Covey **78**
Dirty Gin Martini—Johnny Love's **78**
Gibson Martini—Johnny Love's **80**
Ginseng Martini—Le Colonial **95**
James Bond Martini—The Ritz-Carlton Bar at the
   Ritz-Carlton **96**
Knickerbocker Martini—The Rainbow Room **80**
Manhattan Martini—The Viper Room **114**
Martinez—The Rainbow Room **81**
Melon-Collie—The Mandarin **101**
Melontini—The Lenox Room **102**
Mumbo Martini—Mumbo Jumbo **103**
Park Avenue—Johnny Love's **82**
Perfect Martini—Johnny Love's **82**
Pure Martini—The Ritz-Carlton Bar at the Ritz-Carlton **83**
Red Gin-Gin—The Mandarin **83**
Smokey Martini—Pravda **111**
Supper Martini—Mumbo Jumbo **83**
Thin Man Martini—The Rainbow Room **84**
Very Dirty Martini—Pravda **111**
Vodka Martini—Johnny Love's **108**
Whisky Manhattan—The Martini Club **114**

VODKA

Vodka
Champagne Royale De Martini—Tongue & Groove **88**
Dirty Vodka Martini—Tongue & Groove **92**
French Martini—Pravda **94**
Ginseng Martini—Le Colonial **95**
Grand Martini—Tongue & Groove **96**
Julip Martini—Mason's Restaurant **110**
Lenox Room Peachy Keen Martini—The Lenox
   Room **99**
Litchi Martini—Le Colonial **100**
Melon Martini—Tongue & Groove **101**
Melon-Collie—The Mandarin **101**
Melontini—The Lenox Room **102**
Mint Martini—Pravda **110**
Nutini—Tongue & Groove **103**
Romana Martini—Tongue & Groove **106**
Smokey Martini—Pravda **111**
Sweet Cosmopolitan—Tongue & Groove **107**
The 007 – Shaken, not Stirred—The Viper Room **113**
Tropical Martini—Mason's Restaurant **111**
Truffle Martini—Mason's Restaurant **108**
Very Dirty Martini—Pravda **111**

Absolut Vodka
Absolut Sensation—Compass Rose **85**
Framboise Martini—San Ysidro Ranch **94**
Frangelico Martini—Pravda **94**
Melon Citrus Martini—Pravda **100**
Melon Vodka Martini—Compass Rose **101**

Absolut Citron Vodka
Absolutly Fabulous—The Martini Club **85**
Campton Cosmo—Campton Place Hotel **86**
Campton Cure—Campton Place Hotel **88**
Citrus Martini—Compass Rose **90**
Contemporary—The Covey **90**
Lemon Cosmopolitan—The Martini Club **99**
Lemon Drop Martini—Tongue & Groove **99**
Mr. Phat's Citrus Martini—The Viper Room **102**
Olympic Gold—Garden Court at The Four Seasons
   Olympic Hotel **113**

Absolut Kurant Vodka
Absolutly Fabulous—The Martini Club **85**
Kurant Chocolate Martini—Campton Place Hotel **98**
Kurant Cosmopolitan—Compass Rose **98**
Trai Cay Martini—Le Colonial **108**

Absolut Peppar Vodka
Cajun Martini—Compass Rose **86**
Chesapeake Martini—Explorer's Club **89**

Belvedere Vodka
Double White Chocolate Martini—Mumbo Jumbo **93**
Rainier Martini—Garden Court at The Four Seasons
   Olympic Hotel **105**

Finlandia Vodka
Traditional Martini—Harry Denton's Starlight
   Room **107**

ABOUT THE AUTHOR

Kathleen DeVanna Fish, author of the popular "Secrets" series of cookbooks and guidebooks, is a gourmet cook and gardener who is always on the lookout for recipes with style and character.

In addition to writing *The Elegant Martini,* the native-Californian has written and published over fifteen books, including the award-winning *Great Vegetarian Cookbook* and *Cooking with the Masters of Food and Wine Cookbook.*

Before embarking on a writing and publishing career, she owned and operated three businesses in the travel and hospitality industry.